Adventure Guide to Maine's Abandoned Locomotives

"Ghost Trains" of the Northern Maine Woods

PLEASE NOTE

These maps are the most accurate representation of trail locations possible. Due to the fact that daily changes to driving and trail routes from acts of nature, logging operations, landowner requests, and other unforeseen circumstances are unpredictable, **these maps are not to be used for navigation but for general information only.**

Using this publication means you hold the publisher, property owners, and any other parties who contributed to the creation of this publication harmless for any physical injury or property damage sustained through the use of this publication or these roads and trails. The publisher and all contributors accept absolutely no responsibility for roads and trails being opened or closed, nor the condition of roads or trails.

Please Note: Outdoor adventure and exploration is potentially hazardous. The publisher and author did their best to ensure accuracy of all information at the time of publication, however, they cannot accept responsibility for any loss, injury, or inconvenience experienced by anyone as a result of information or advice in this book. Also, land ownership, roads and trails change over time. If you discover changes in ownership, roads, trails, or any other inaccurate information please let us know so we can correct it for future editions. The author and publisher also welcome any comments or suggestions.

Contact us at:
Untamed Mainer
PO Box 93
Little Deer Isle, ME 04650
Ang@UntamedMainer.com

Please Help Keep
Maine's Wilderness Untamed!

TABLE OF CONTENTS

The Abandoned Locomotives and Tramway Historic District are part of the Allagash Wilderness Waterway

All artifacts here belong to the State of Maine Allagash Wilderness Waterway. **The disturbance, retrieval, or posession of any artifacts is prohibited and there are fines of up to $500 for violations of these rules.** The fantastic Rangers who work for the Allagash Wilderness Waterway frequently visit and maintain this site for preservation purposes as well as your safety and enjoyment. *Please help them by leaving things as you found them and by carrying in/carrying out your trash and any that may have been left by others.*

Please follow these rules so many more generations of children and adults can enjoy the Abandoned Locomotives and Tramway Historic District just as you did!

A Brief History of Tramway Historic District

Lumbering has long been a part of Maine's history, and lumbermen faced many obstacles moving logs over Maine's unique and challenging terrain. These were overcome with creative ingenuity which can still be seen today throughout our state. There were two separate operations that took place at Tramway Historic District. The first was Tramway Village, operated from 1902-1907. The second was the Eagle Lake and West Branch Railroad, which operated from 1926-1933. There is much conflicting information about the lumbering history of this region. The history that follows is based on the most accurate information from credible, reliable sources available at the time of print.

Telos Cut

At the southern end of Chamberlain Lake lies Telos Lake. A small section of land between Telos Lake and Webster Lake was the only separation between the headwaters of the Allagash River, which flows south to north into Canada, and the East Branch Penobscot River, which flows north to south into Bangor. Three men from Bangor, Amos Roberts, and brothers S.P. Strickland and Hastings Strickland bought the entire area surrounding the two small lakes in 1838 and came up with a way to reverse the natural flow of Chamberlain Lake to move Maine's logs south towards Millinocket and Bangor to support American interests.

The men first built a dam at the outlet of Chamberlain Lake to raise the water level to a second dam built at Telos Lake. These two dams raised the water level almost as high as Webster Lake. In 1841 a canal between Telos Lake and Webster Lake was constructed, now known as "Telos Cut," measuring just 10-15 feet wide and around 1-4 feet deep. This series of dams and the canal made it possible for all timber harvested in the Chamberlain Lake region to be driven south into the East Branch Penobscot River.

This system was not flawless. It spurred the "Telos War" after Amos Roberts bought out the Strickland brothers and began charging a 50 cent toll per thousand board feet for using the canal. Next, the dam washed out at Chamberlain Lake which made the canal useless so Roberts decided to sell it to Rufus Dwinel. Dwinel had the Chamberlain Dam rebuilt, and in 1846 he blocked off the canal and hired 75 men to guard it. When lumbermen encountered the barrier they had to sign an agreement to pay both the toll and an additional amount to cover the cost of maintaining Dwinel's guards.

This became very expensive and lumbermen went to the Maine legislature for help. Dwinel was given an ultimatum of reducing the toll to 10 cents or incorporating his business and cut the toll. He agreed to the second option and established the Telos Canal Company and reduced the toll to 20 cents.

Tramway Village, 1902-1907

Engineer Fred Dow was commissioned to design a tramway system powered by steam in 1902 for lumbermen Herbert W. Marsh and Frederick W. Ayer. This would make it possible to move logs between the shores of Eagle Lake to Chamberlain Lake without the need to use a lock dam system which was presently in use. Once in Chamberlain Lake, logs were driven south through Telos Cut. A small village was set up at the site for the lumbermen and even included a post office which was a popular meeting place for workers.

A majority of the parts to construct the tramway were transported through the summer and fall of 1901. They were brought by railroad to Greenville Junction then taken by boat across Moosehead Lake to North East Carry. Horsepower was used to transport the parts the rest of the way to Chesuncook Lake and over Mud Pond Carry to their present site between Eagle and Chamberlain Lakes. H.N. Bartley hauled the remaining parts over the winter of 1901-1902. This included a continuous section of cable that measured 6,000 feet long. Teams of horses were used to drag the skids that carried the cable but the process was slow and exhausting. Only a short way from Moosehead Lake at Smith's Camp on the West Branch Penobscot River the decision was made to cut the cable in half. It was spliced back together at Tramway Village, and the splice can still be seen today.

Construction of the Tramway was completed in 1903 with operations beginning that spring. The Tramway worked like a conveyor system. A graded railroad bed was constructed between the shores of Eagle Lake and Chamberlain Lake. Next, the 6,000-foot cable was stretched along the bed with the top of the cable running in between a 22-inch gauge track sitting on timber supports and the bottom section supported with cedar ties creating a conveyor belt. Six hundred two-wheeled steel "trucks" with two metal toothed plates to grip the logs rode on the tracks and clamps that fit into the drive sprocket wheel were placed along the cable every 5 feet to help the sprocket grip the cable (see image below).

ABOVE: Tramway cable and trucks hauling timber on wooden supports. Note the returning truck on the bottom. LEFT: Drive sprocket and engine house that powered the Tramway.

The conveyor system was pulled by a drive sprocket at the Chamberlain Lake end that measured 9 feet in diameter. The system was powered by a two-cylinder Westinghouse Compound Steam Engine designed for electric light plants and had a 12-inch and 24-inch cylinder with a fourteen-inch stroke. It ran at 255rpm with 100 pounds of steam pressure. The steam was supplied by two wood-fired Hodge boilers. Logs were loaded onto the steel trucks on the upper level of the conveyor at the Eagle Lake end and were pulled 3,000 feet and dumped into Chamberlain Lake at the other end. From there they were floated down the lake to Telos Cut and then to Bangor. Once the steel truck released the log it would continue back towards the Eagle Lake end upside down on the lower level.

During the first test run of the conveyor system workers realized the cable was slipping. None of the bolts used to hold the 600 trucks and 600 clamps were tight enough as the threads were too short. They had to remove all 4,800 bolts and make the threads longer using a hand die, then put each one back into place. The second time the conveyor system was fired up workers were disappointed to see that the system didn't move nearly as fast as it was supposed to. The first few logs finally passed over a high rise in the ground and when they reached the downward slope on the other side their weight caused the system to pick up speed. Workers were relieved to see that all of their hard work had paid off- the system was running just as expected.

When operating at full steam the Tramway could move half a million board feet per day operating at around 3mph from 4 am to 8 pm, 7 days per week. When the system wasn't running, workers would maintain the track and tighten bolts. Logs were supplied by loggers who cut and hauled long logs in the winter by horses and sleds which were piled up on the ice and shores of Eagle Lake. A side wheel steamboat, H.W. Marsh, was custom built to boom and tow the logs to Tramway after ice-out. Parts of the H.W. Marsh can still be seen today at Chamberlain Farm. Once the logs crossed the Tramway and were dumped into Chamberlain Lake another steamboat, the George A. Dugan, would boom and tow the logs down to Telos Lake.

At the end of 1907, Ayer decided the entire process was outdated since horses were limited in the speed and distance they could haul loads by sled. He abandoned Tramway Village and purchased Lombard Log Haulers, invented by a man from Waterville, Maine.

In 1901, Alvin O. Lombard built the first Lombard Steam Log Hauler to replace the need for draft horses to haul heavy loads through the woods. They were a continuous-tread tractor with no brakes yet were incredibly effective. They were used to plow roads, haul water to ice the roads, and worked as dump trucks. Some were designed with wheels on the front, and others had skis to go through the snow. Lombard only made 83 tractors in his lifetime, and the American Society of Mechanical Engineers recognized the Lombard Log Hauler as a National Historic Mechanical Engineering Landmark.

Unlike horses, Lombards were powerful enough to haul multiple sleds loaded with logs from deep within the woods throughout the winter. Well maintained woods roads were constructed leading directly to the shores of Chamberlain Lake. The timber was unloaded onto the ice and then driven down the lake through Telos Cut to the East Branch Penobscot River after ice-out. Ayer continued logging operations in the region using his Lombard Log Haulers for many years.

Today the only remaining parts of the Tramway that can be seen are the tracks, trucks, clamps and steel cable that runs alongside the portage trail between Eagle Lake and Chamberlain Lake, and parts of the power plant near the shore of Chamberlain Lake including the large sprocket, the Westinghouse compound engine, and the two Hodge boilers.

Eagle Lake and West Branch Railroad, 1926-1933

Tramway remained a ghost town until it was sold to Edouard "King" Lacroix who wanted to replace the Tramway with a forest railway system to haul timbers from the shores of Eagle Lake, over Chamberlain Lake (Chamberlain Arm), directly to Umbazooksus Lake. From there, logs could be driven south through Chesuncook Lake which connects to the West Branch Penobscot River and mills in Millinocket.

During the winter of 1926, he began hauling materials to build what he called the **Umbazooksus and Eagle Lake Railroad** from Lac Frontier, Quebec, to Churchill Depot. Next, he hauled the railway equipment over the ice of Churchill Lake to the shore of Eagle Lake. He used Lombard Log Haulers to move the materials and is know to have purchased more of Alvin Lombard's tractors than any other lumberman.

The Lombard Log Haulers brought miles of steel rail, two Plymouth gasoline-powered switchers, and sixty railroad cars designed to carry pulpwood. The railroad cars measured 32 feet long, had high sides built with slats, and could hold 12 cords of wood each. The tractors also delivered the two 100-ton steam locomotives that still remain at the site today. Engine #1 was built by Schenectady Locomotive Works in 1897, and Engine #2 was built by Brooks Locomotive Works in 1901. Both locomotives were converted from coal-burning to oil burning because coal can cause forest fires from the cinders.

Lacroix used a steam-powered shovel to build a 13-mile railroad bed from the shore of Eagle Lake down to Umbazooksus Lake. A bucket from one of these shovels and some of the flatbed cars used to build the bed can be seen today. They are located just beyond the large boiler tank you pass on the trail to the trains. He also had to build a 1,500-foot wooden trestle to cross the north end of Chamberlain Lake, known as Chamberlain Arm, part of which can still be seen today. The tracks were standard gauge 4-feet, 8.5 inches.

Lacroix built three 40hp diesel-powered conveyors to lift the logs from Eagle Lake. Each conveyor was 225 feet long and raised the logs a total of 25 feet to reach the height of the railroad cars. One conveyor could move one cord of wood in a minute and a half, filling the 12 cord cars in just 18 minutes. The floor of each pulpwood car was tilted 6 inches, and the tracks that extended 600 feet into Umbazooksus Lake were also tilted 6 inches so when the pins were removed from the hinged side of the car the logs would fall out into the lake without the need for equipment to unload them.

Despite all of his hard work, Lacroix never actually operated the railroad. On June 1st, 1927 he sold it to Great Northern Paper Company (GNP) who renamed it the **Eagle Lake and West Branch Railroad (EL & WB RR)**. The railroad operated 24 hours a day from ice out to when the lakes froze.

Both locomotives rotated hauling 10-12 pulpwood cars from Eagle Lake to Umbazooksus Lake, and when returning the empty cars they would carry supplies back for lumbering operation and lumbermen including drums of fuel for the locomotives, conveyors, and switchers. Each round trip took around 3 hours to complete, and a passing track in the middle of the route made it possible for both locomotives to operate without interruption.

The only time the locomotives would stop was after returning with empty cars. They would sit for 10 minutes for service by the workers. At that time, a smaller Plymouth engine would move the next set of filled pulpwood cars to a location where the locomotive could connect to them, and move the empty cars under the conveyors to be loaded. In just one year the locomotives would haul an average of 65,000 cord of wood, moving over 6,500 cord of wood in an average week.

So what happened to the railroad operation and why did the locomotives get abandoned in the woods?

During the Great Depression, the demand for paper dropped significantly, eventually causing operations to cease in 1933. By then the locomotives had become obsolete and the cost was too high to bring them out of the woods. They were parked in the very location you see them in today. An engine house originally covered the locomotives but in 1969, through a miscommunication, the Maine Forest Service was told to burn all wooden structures except the engine house but burned it as well which destroyed the wooden cab on Engine #1.

A Brief History of Tramway Historic District

Although the railroad operation was abandoned, the Maine Forest Service maintained a forest service camp at Tramway Village for many years. In the 1960's Fire Warden Frank Emerson overhauled a gas engine of an old railroad car once used to carry workers over the tracks and attached it to a small railroad car known as a "pede." He used it for fast (and apparently very fun!) transportation between the shores of Eagle Lake and Chamberlain Lake over the abandoned train tracks so he could patrol both lakes for fires. Eventually, Fire Wardens no longer stayed at the site and it became completely abandoned, with Albert Thibodeau being the last Maine Forest Service Ranger to live and work at what was then known as Eagle Lake Village.

Today we can still see many objects that paint a picture of a once booming lumbering industry that took place here. The locomotives are by far the most impressive sight.
Other points of interest include:
- Tramway which follows along the portage path between Eagle and Chamberlain Lake
- Boiler, cogs and pulley system of the engine house that powered the system on the Chamberlain Lake side
- Abandoned pulpwood cars
- Boarding house foundation (where workers stayed)
- Well
- Flagpole from Fire Warden camp
- Tons other metal objects which formed either part of the Tramway or the Eagle Lake & West Branch Railroad scattered throughout the area

Tramway Village and the Eagle Lake & West Branch Railroad were both awesome industrial feats. Engineered through ingenuity, the infrastructure delivered through determination and incredible problem solving, and assembled, operated and maintained by lumbermen who formed the heart and history of lumbering in Maine.

A clear section of the Tramway showing trucks, the steel cable, and rails in the woods.

Make sure you are prepared, especially in the colder months!

* The drive in on the logging roads can be VERY hazardous! Flat tires are EXTREMELY common on logging roads (I've had one!). Logging roads are typically covered in broken shale, which means there is a high risk of getting a flat tire from driving on these roads- especially near the edges of the road. Don't count on someone coming by to change your flat tire for you- the logging trucks are working and can't stop and traffic on these roads is very unpredictable and changes throughout the year. Due to these factors it is HIGHLY recommended that you bring the following items:

1. TWO spare tires (yes, 2!)
2. Jack and tire iron, cheater bar for tire iron if needed
3. Tire pump (invest in a good one, as cheaper ones burn out easily!)
4. Tire repair kit with pressure gauge
5. Fix-a-flat of some kind
6. Someone in the vehicle that can change a flat tire if you get one!

* **LOGGING TRUCKS ALWAYS HAVE RIGHT OF WAY.** These roads are not state-owned, they are owned by many different logging companies. Logging roads are dirt roads and are built for tractor-trailer trucks loaded with tree length logs to move timber out of the woods and to the mill. They use these roads almost DAILY hauling logs and they <u>drive just as fast on dirt logging roads as they do on paved ones!</u> They are very heavy and cannot maneuver or stop quickly to go out around you. **ALWAYS pull to the right out of the way whenever you encounter a logging truck, and pull over if one comes up behind you and let them by.**

* Low-clearance vehicles may bottom out on the logging roads depending on conditions.

* Logging roads are VERY dusty during the dry season. Make sure you have extra washer fluid in your vehicle and be prepared to have some dust on the inside of your vehicle (and TONS on the outside of it!).

* When the logging trucks aren't going by, moose and deer own the roads. Watch out for them, because they may not be watching out for you. Slow down and don't chase any moose you see, as they could charge your vehicle if you do.

* There aren't many identifying road name signs on the logging roads, so don't be surprised if you don't see any.

* Some sections of the dirt roads have LOTS of potholes that you cannot avoid. Be prepared to drive REALLY slow in these sections, especially after you pass the parking lot at Chamberlain Lake all the way to the trains parking lot.

* You MUST stop at Telos Checkpoint and pay a fee to use these roads. **The fee is $11 for Maine residents and $16 for non-residents for day use.** Under 18 and over 70 are free, but still must check in.

* Bring extra food and water, a blanket and layers of warm clothing in case you break down or have a flat you can't fix and get stuck on the side of the road for an extended period of time or overnight.

* Once you go above Kokadjo or reach the Golden Road, depending on which way you are coming from, your

cell phone will be good for telling the time and taking pictures…that's about it.

* If you're planning on going during mud season (spring), you may want to change your plans. Or make sure your vehicle has a winch on the front of it. The mud can get REALLY deep in some areas from flooding/standing water.

*If you go during blackfly season (late mud season through mid summer), you are definitely going to want to bring some bug spray. Trust me on this one.

* There is a LOT of wildlife in this area, and they use these trails too! It isn't uncommon to see signs of deer, moose, and bear in this region. They are more afraid of you than you are of them, but they can attack if you surprise them. Because of this, you should bring some bear spray and do your best to make a good deal of noise as you travel through the woods. This will alert the wildlife to your presence and they will most likely run away. Be aware that GUNS ARE NOT PERMITTED within the 1-mile zone of the Allagash Wilderness Waterway where the Abandoned Locomotives are located. Bear spray and lots of noise, my friends.

* The hiking trail in can be muddy any season depending on recent rainfall. Bring footwear that can get wet (NOT SANDALS!) and a good change of socks.

AREA DAY TRIPS &
NATURAL ATTRACTIONS

Have some time to spare and want more adventure? Check out these awesome area side trips:

Ripogenus Gorge, 45.877670, -69.139458
Deep gorge the West Branch Penobscot River cuts through, incredible views.

Abol Bridge, 45.835310, -68.968125
Highly scenic bridge spanning the West Branch Penobscot River with breathtaking views of Mt. Katahdin.

Debsconeag Ice Caves- Moderate hike of around 30 minutes leads to caves often filled with ice even in the summer. Metal rung ladders lead down into the caves, bring a flashlight! The road to the ice caves is clearly marked just after crossing Abol Bridge.

Baxter State Park- Ride around the loop road or stop for a couple of nice hikes, including two nearby waterfall hikes, Big Niagara Falls and Katahdin Stream Falls.

Ripogenus Gorge

View from Abol Bridge

Debsconeag Ice Caves

Katahdin Stream Falls

Location of Maine's Abandoned Ghost Trains
Eagle Lake Township, T8, R13 WELS
DeLorme: Map 55, D5 | GPS: 46.322469, -69.375147

How to Understand these Directions:

"Bear to the right" means there are two roads in front of you, including the one you are on, and you want to stay on the road in the direction that is to your right. This could be considered "straight," but I'm calling it "right." In the photo above, there is a road that goes to the left and the one you are on. They both look the same and it is hard to tell which one is the main road. In this case, I would say "bear to the right" (aka "go straight") There are very few road signs on logging roads!

I have also listed CHECKPOINTS to look for so you know you are on the right track. If a checkpoint is a sign, that does NOT mean go that way! It just means that you see the sign, and therefore are on the right road. Please be advised that signs blow down from the weather, or could have been removed since these directions were published. If you do not see a checkpoint sign that does not necessarily mean you are on the wrong road. Look for the next checkpoint and check your map! (Always bring a map).

Map from GREENVILLE/KOKADJO TO THE ABANDONED LOCOMOTIVES

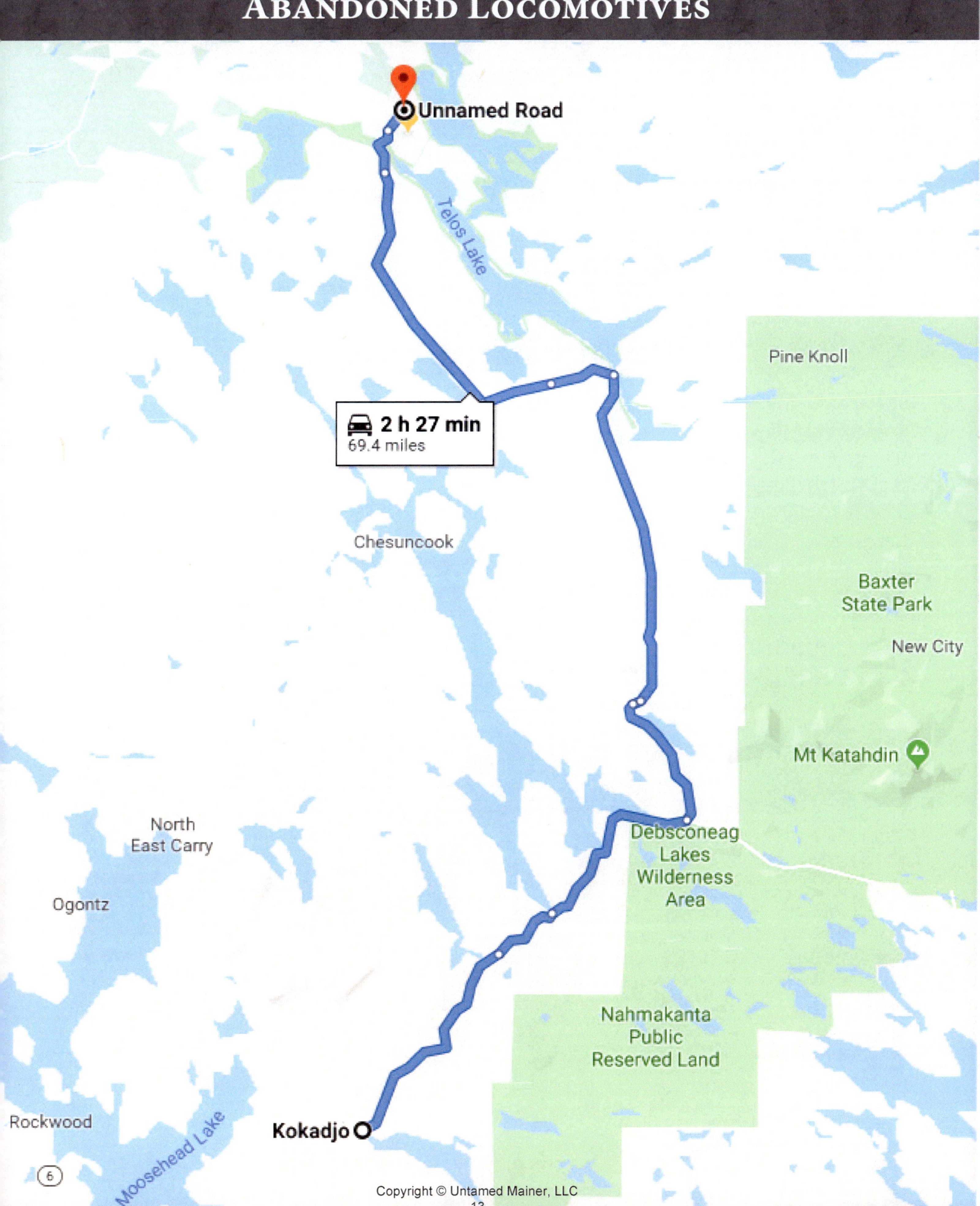

Turn-By-Turn Driving Directions from Greenville/Kokadjo

1. **[DeLORME MAP 41]** Drive to the small town of Kokadjo, just north of Greenville.
2. The pavement will end in Kokadjo right after the pond and the general store and turn to dirt.
3. Take a left where the pavement ends and you will be on Sias Hill Road. (Going right will put you on North Shore Road.)
4. Bear to the right (NOT towards Spencer Camps, which are on Spencer Bay Road.)
5. Stay on the main road, NOT the road to the sporting camps which is on Smithtown Road.
6. **CHECKPOINT**: Plum Creek Sign.
7. Continue going straight, not towards Sias Hill Cutoff Road.
8. **[DeLORME MAP 49]** Drive through the large yellow pillars.
9. **CHECKPOINT**: One lane bridge.
10. Go forward past road to Big Spencer Mountain Trail (Spencer Mountain Road).
11. **[DeLORME MAP 50]** **CHECKPOINT**: Ragged Riders sign and Ragged Lake East Bridge on your left.
12. **CHECKPOINT**: One lane bridge then a "Stop Ahead" sign.
13. When you come to the end of the road and stop sign you will take a right onto Golden Road. There is no sign that shows you have reached Golden Road, just a whole bunch of hunting camp and lodge signs.
14. **CHECKPOINT**: Pavement!
15. **CHECKPOINT**: Driving past Chesuncook Lake, you will see a driftwood beach.
16. **CHECKPOINT**: The road becomes a mix of pavement and dirt.
17. **CHECKPOINT**: Allagash Gateway Cabins sign.
18. **CHECKPOINT**: Drive past the road to Frost Pond Camps
19. **CHECKPOINT**: Power lines.
20. **NATURAL LANDMARK**: There is a turnout near the power lines- pull in here and look for a trail. Just a short walk and you will see the beautiful Ripogenus Gorge!
21. The road will divide- go LEFT onto Telos Road.
22. **CHECKPOINT**: Ladd Hill.
23. **CHECKPOINT**: Gravel pit
24. **CHECKPOINT**: You will see a mountain to your left (Soubunge Mountain)
25. **TELOS CHECKPOINT**: You must stop at the Telos Checkpoint and give them your personal information.
26. There is a fee of $11 per person for Mainers and $16 per person for everyone else to use the Telos Road. When you return you must again stop at Telos Checkpoint to let them know you are leaving the area. **DETAILED MAPS FROM THE TELOS CHECKPOINT TO THE TRAILHEAD PARKING LOT START ON PAGE 19**
27. **CHECKPOINT**: White and red mile marker signs, Marker 48
28. Go past Telos Mountain Road which will be on your right.
29. **[DeLORME MAP 56]**

30. CHECKPOINT: Allagash Wilderness Waterway sign, Chamberlain Bridge and Ranger Station

31. If you look at the map, it looks like the road will come to a "T" stop and you will be able to choose left or right, which is at the bottom of Chamberlain Lake. In reality, the main road (Telos Road) will take a sharp right where a rest stop area lies in front of you. It really is a rest stop, fully equipped with porta-potties! Great place to take a quick break, and when you reach this point, you need to turn LEFT off of Telos Road and onto Guy Allen Road/Longley Stream Road. Again, don't bother looking for road signs, because there aren't any.

32. [DeLORME MAP 50]

33. CHECKPOINT: The road will become more narrow (and rougher!).

34. [DeLORME MAP 49]

35. Take a RIGHT at the fork onto Grand Marche Road. You will see a "Trans Canada" sign, but no sign for Grand Marche Road.

36. [DeLORME MAP 55]

37. CHECKPOINT: Sharp 90 degree corner and a Johnson Allagash Lodge sign. There is a sign that says you are on Edmond Roy Road.

38. CHECKPOINT: Mile marker 21.

39. CHECKPOINT: One lane bridge (over Upper Deadwater/Ellis Brook)

40. CHECKPOINT: Continue on main road, do NOT turn left onto Ledge Road, heading towards Loon Lodge.

41. CHECKPOINT: West Road will be to your left and Chamberlain Lake Road will be to your right, stay on the main road.

42. CHECKPOINT: Logging camp.

43. CHECKPOINT: Mile marker 15

44. CHECKPOINT: Crossing over Allagash Stream, Allagash Wilderness Waterway sign.

45. Not far past the Allagash Stream crossing you'll see a sign pointing to the right that reads Tramway Road. Turn right onto Tramway Road.

46. Follow Tramway Road for another 1.2 miles and you will see another right hand turn with a sign that reads Tramway. Turn right on this road.

47. This road is VERY rough with lots of potholes and lasts another 1.5 miles.

48. YOU HAVE ARRIVED! GPS Coordinates at Parking Area: 46°19.643'N, 069°23.413'W Google Maps hasn't figured out that a road leads to this location, so **don't use Google Map Directions to get here!** This is more for reference.

49. The dirt parking lot is HUGE and has plenty of room for quite a few vehicles. There is a nice new wooden outhouse at the edge of the parking area that even had toilet paper in it when I visited, but I would bring some along just in case. The trailhead is very obvious and clearly marked at the far edge of the parking area which you will notice when you first pull in.

Map from Medway/Millinocket Area to the Abandoned Locomotives

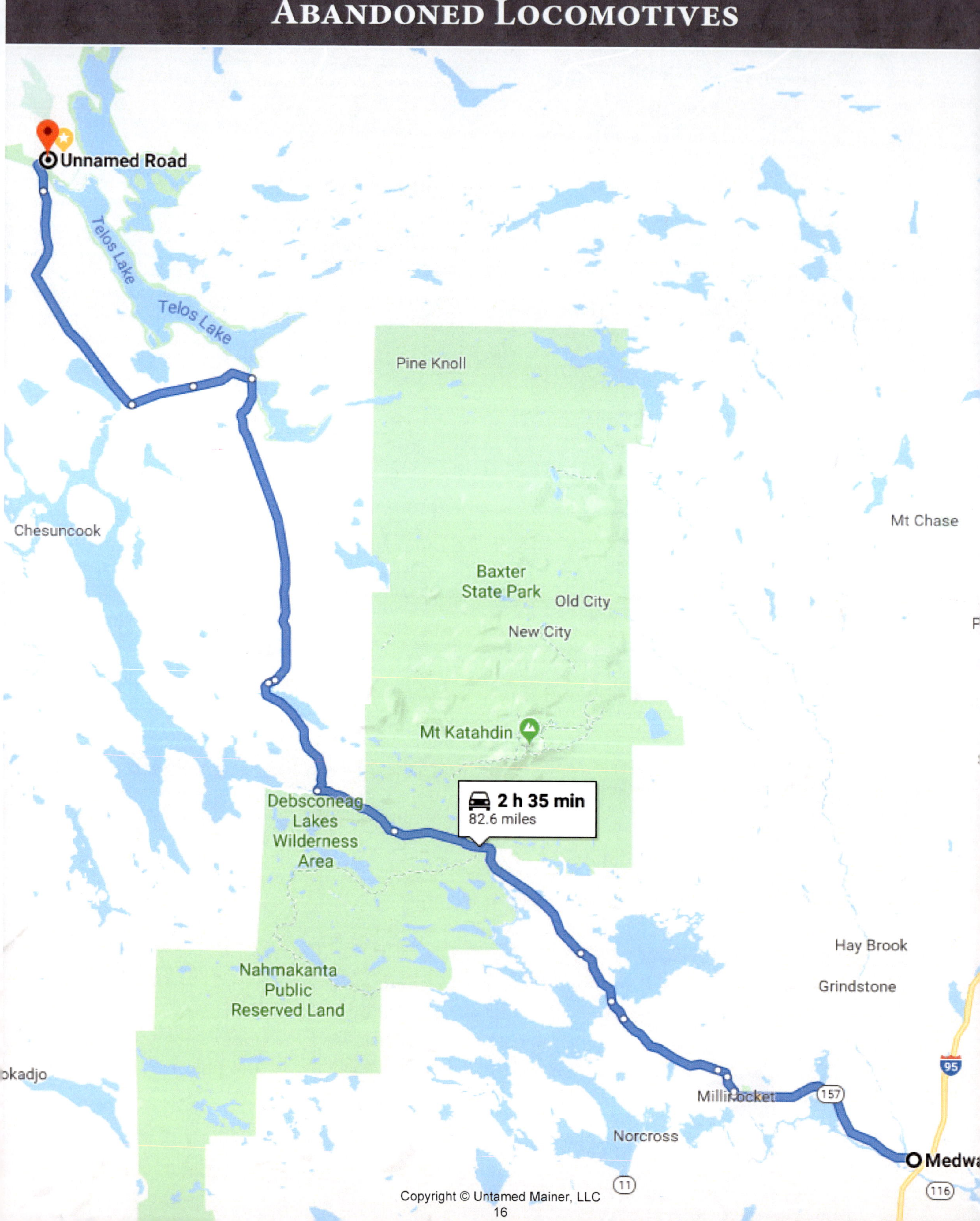

Turn-By-Turn Driving Directions from Medway/Millinocket

1. **[DeLORME MAP 43]** Follow I-95 to the Medway/Millinocket exit number 244
2. Take Route 11/157 into Millinocket. From here you have several options, all which work fine. You can take the Golden Road from the beginning which starts just above Ferguson Lake just outside of the town of Millinocket, or you can take Millinocket Lake Road which leads to Baxter Park Road which starts in town, which is the way I prefer. Since it is the way I prefer these are the directions I'll use.
3. Stay on **Route 157 W** for about 10.7 miles
4. Follow the signs for Baxter State Park. Turn right on **Katahdin Avenue**.
5. This goes a short ways then you turn left at the second cross street to **Bates Street**.
6. In just under a mile you'll reach **Millinocket Road** which eventually becomes **Millinocket Lake Road**.
7. **NOTE**: This road runs right beside the Golden Road for quite some miles. If you're eager to get dirt under your tires, feel free to take one of these side roads to the Golden Road at any point. It all leads to the same place. If you'd rather stick to the more "maintained for passenger vehicles" dirt road, which also could minimize your chance of a flat tire, follow the directions below!
8. Once you drive between Millinocket Lake and Ambajejus Lake you'll be on Baxter Park Road. In about 3 miles you'll see a left hand turn towards the Golden Road, take that, then take a right onto the Golden Road.
9. Follow the Golden Road for approximately 16.5 miles, then take a right onto Telos Road.
10. CHECKPOINT: Ladd Hill.
11. CHECKPOINT: Gravel pit
12. CHECKPOINT: You will see a mountain to your left (Soubunge Mountain)
13. **TELOS CHECKPOINT**: You must stop at the Telos Checkpoint and give them your personal information. There is a fee of $11 per person for Mainers and $16 per person for everyone else to use the Telos Road. When you return you must again stop at Telos Checkpoint to let them know you are leaving the area. **DETAILED MAPS FROM THE TELOS CHECKPOINT TO THE TRAILHEAD PARKING LOT START ON PAGE 19**
14. CHECKPOINT: White and red mile marker signs, Marker 48
15. Go past Telos Mountain Road which will be on your right.
16. **[DeLORME MAP 56]**
17. **CHECKPOINT: Allagash Wilderness Waterway sign, Chamberlain Bridge and Ranger Station**
18. If you look at the map, it looks like the road will come to a "T" stop and you will be able to choose left or right, which is at the bottom of Chamberlain Lake. In reality, the

main road (Telos Road) will take a sharp right where a rest stop area lies in front of you. It really is a rest stop, fully equipped with porta-potties! Great place to take a quick break, and when you reach this point, you need to turn LEFT off of Telos Road and onto Guy Allen Road/Longley Stream Road. Again, don't bother looking for road signs, because there aren't any.

19. [DeLORME MAP 50]

20. CHECKPOINT: The road will become more narrow (and rougher!).

21. [DeLORME MAP 49]

22. Take a RIGHT at the fork onto Grand Marche Road. You will see a "Trans Canada" sign, but no sign for Grand Marche Road.

23. [DeLORME MAP 55]

24. CHECKPOINT: Sharp 90 degree corner and a Johnson Allagash Lodge sign. There is a sign that says you are on Edmond Roy Road.

25. CHECKPOINT: Mile marker 21.

26. CHECKPOINT: One lane bridge (over Upper Deadwater/Ellis Brook)

27. CHECKPOINT: Continue on main road, do NOT turn left onto Ledge Road, heading towards Loon Lodge.

28. CHECKPOINT: West Road will be to your left and Chamberlain Lake Road will be to your right, stay on the main road.

29. CHECKPOINT: Logging camp.

30. CHECKPOINT: Mile marker 15

31. CHECKPOINT: Crossing over Allagash Stream, Allagash Wilderness Waterway sign.

32. Not far past the Allagash Stream crossing you'll see a sign pointing to the right that reads Tramway Road. Turn right onto Tramway Road.

33. Follow Tramway Road for another 1.2 miles and you will see another right hand turn with a sign that reads Tramway. Turn right on this road.

34. This road is VERY rough with lots of potholes and lasts another 1.5 miles.

35. YOU HAVE ARRIVED! GPS Coordinates at Parking Area: 46°19.643'N, 069°23.413'W Google Maps hasn't figured out that a road leads to this location, so **don't use Google Map Directions to get here!** This is more for reference.

36. The dirt parking lot is HUGE and has plenty of room for quite a few vehicles. There is a nice new wooden outhouse at the edge of the parking area that even had toilet paper in it when I visited, but I would bring some along just in case. The trailhead is very obvious and clearly marked at the far edge of the parking area which you will notice when you first pull in.

Detailed Map & Driving Directions from Telos Checkpoint to the Abandoned Locomotives Trailhead Parking Lot

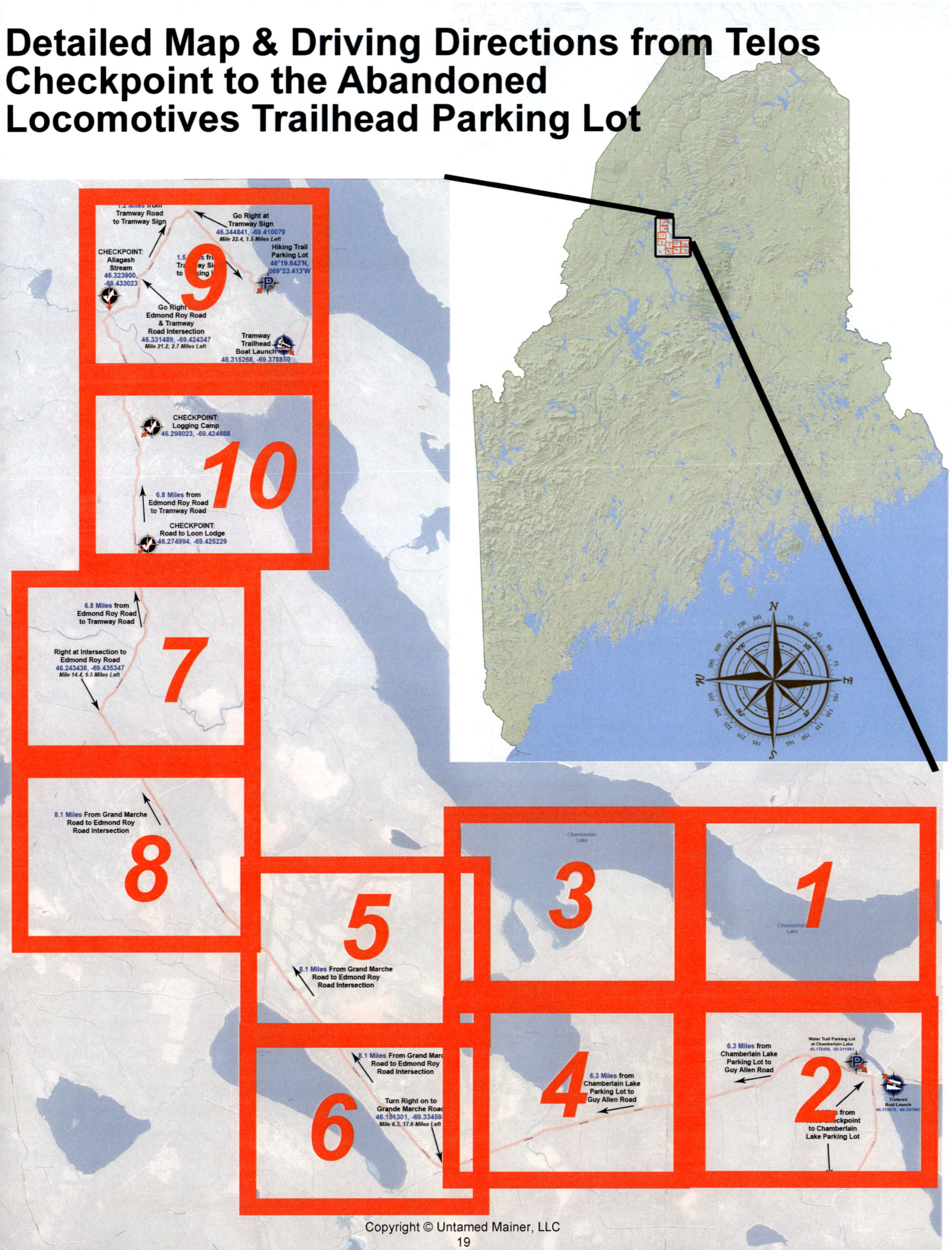

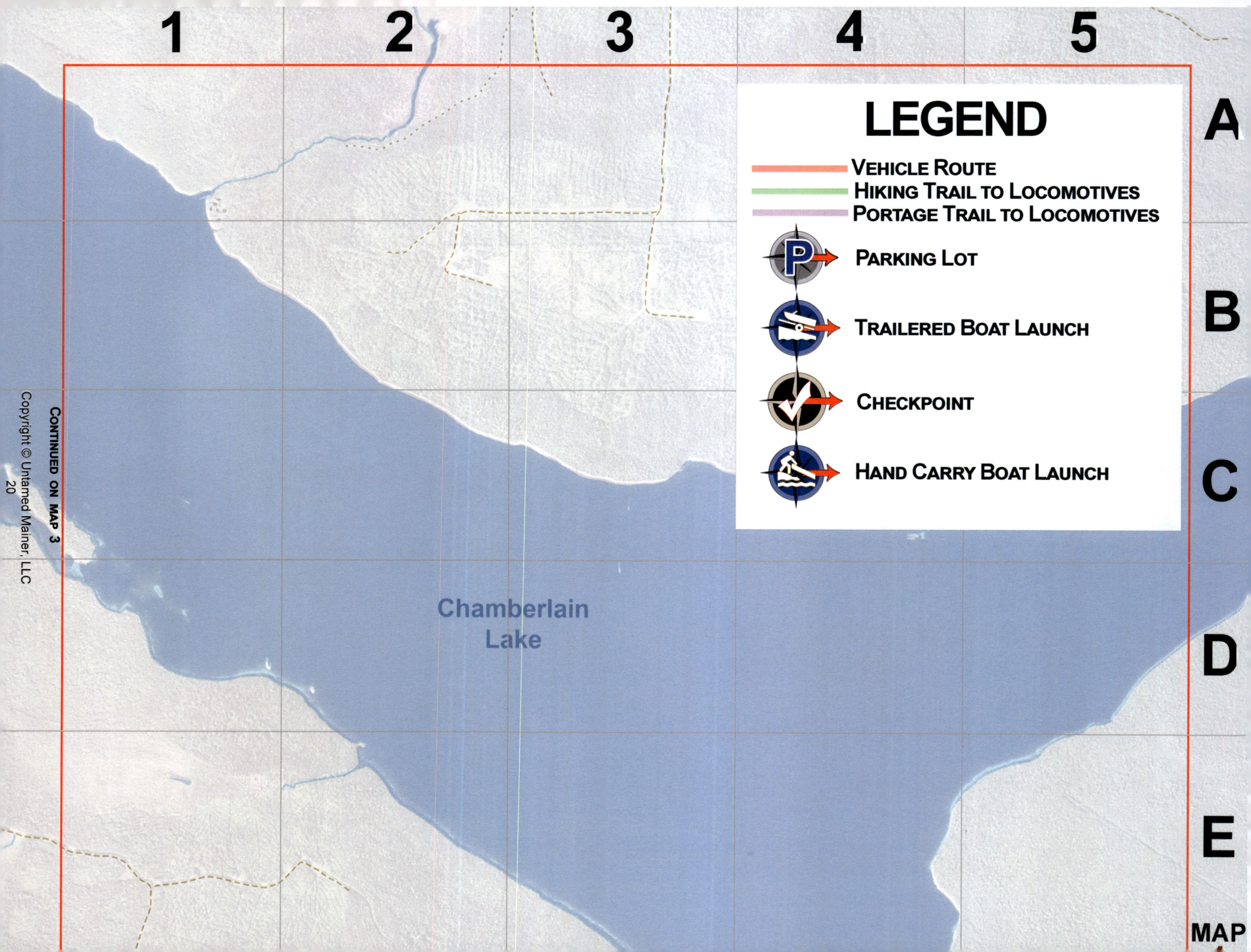

1
2
3
4
5
A
B
C
D
E
MAP
LEGEND
Vehicle Route
Hiking Trail to Locomotives
Portage Trail to Locomotives
Parking Lot
Trailered Boat Launch
Checkpoint
Hand Carry Boat Launch
Chamberlain Lake
Continued on Map 3
Copyright © Untamed Mainer, LLC
20

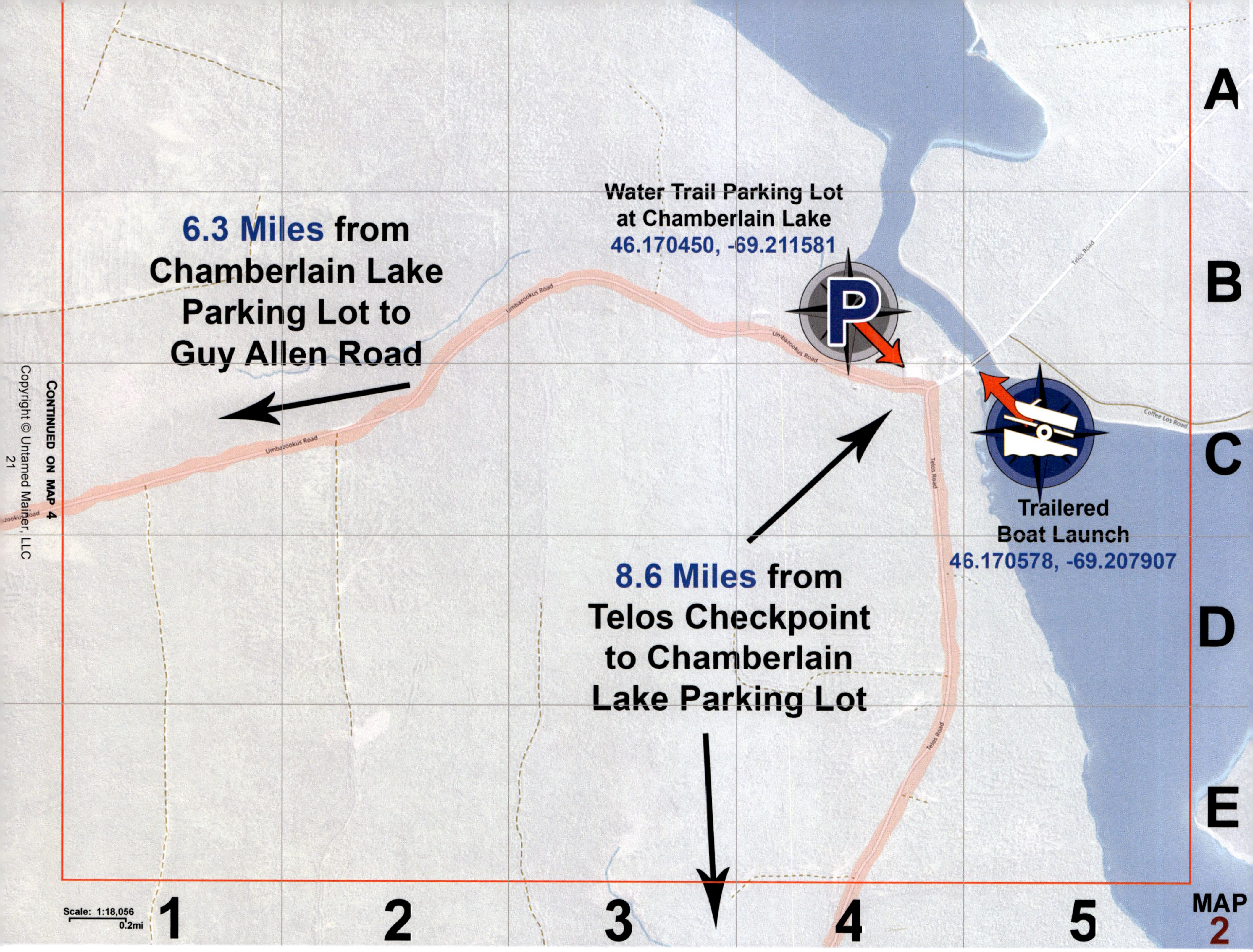

CONTINUED ON MAP 4

21

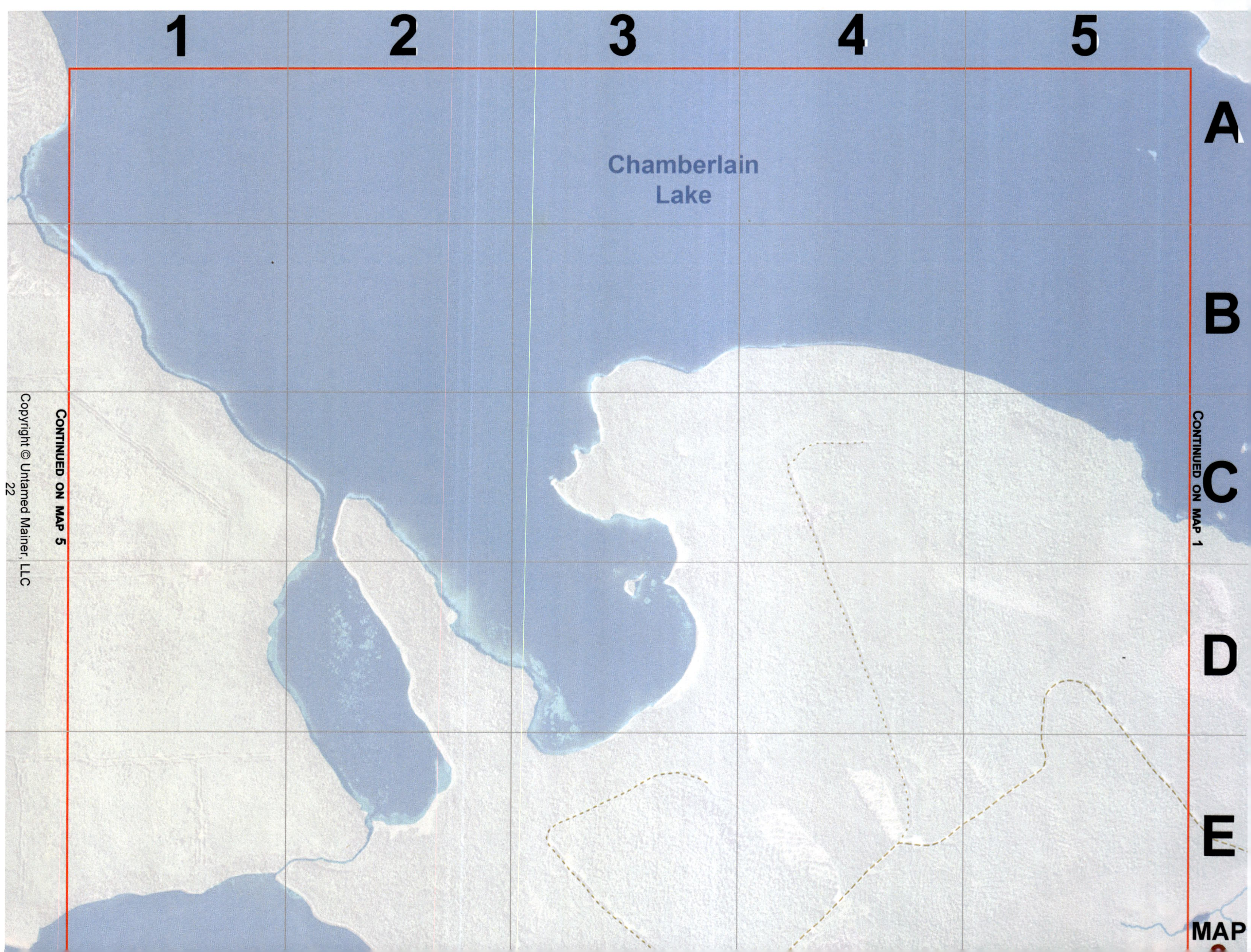

1
2
3
4
5
A
B
C
D
E
MAP
Chamberlain Lake
CONTINUED ON MAP 5
CONTINUED ON MAP 1

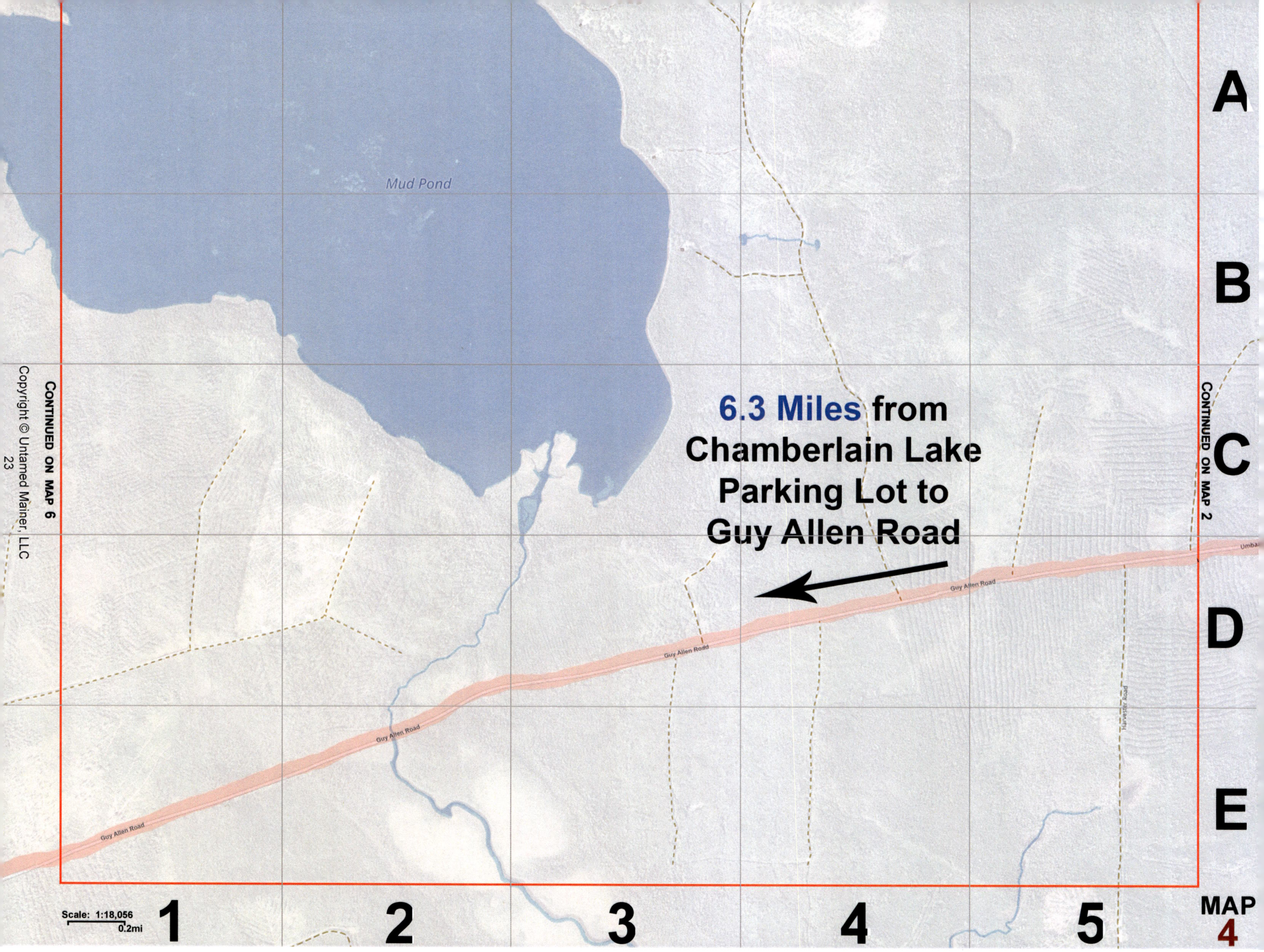
6.3 Miles from
Chamberlain Lake
Parking Lot to
Guy Allen Road
Mud Pond
Guy Allen Road
Harvester Road
Umbazooksus
MAP 4
Scale: 1:18,056
0.2mi
A B C D E
1 2 3 4 5
CONTINUED ON MAP 2
CONTINUED ON MAP 6

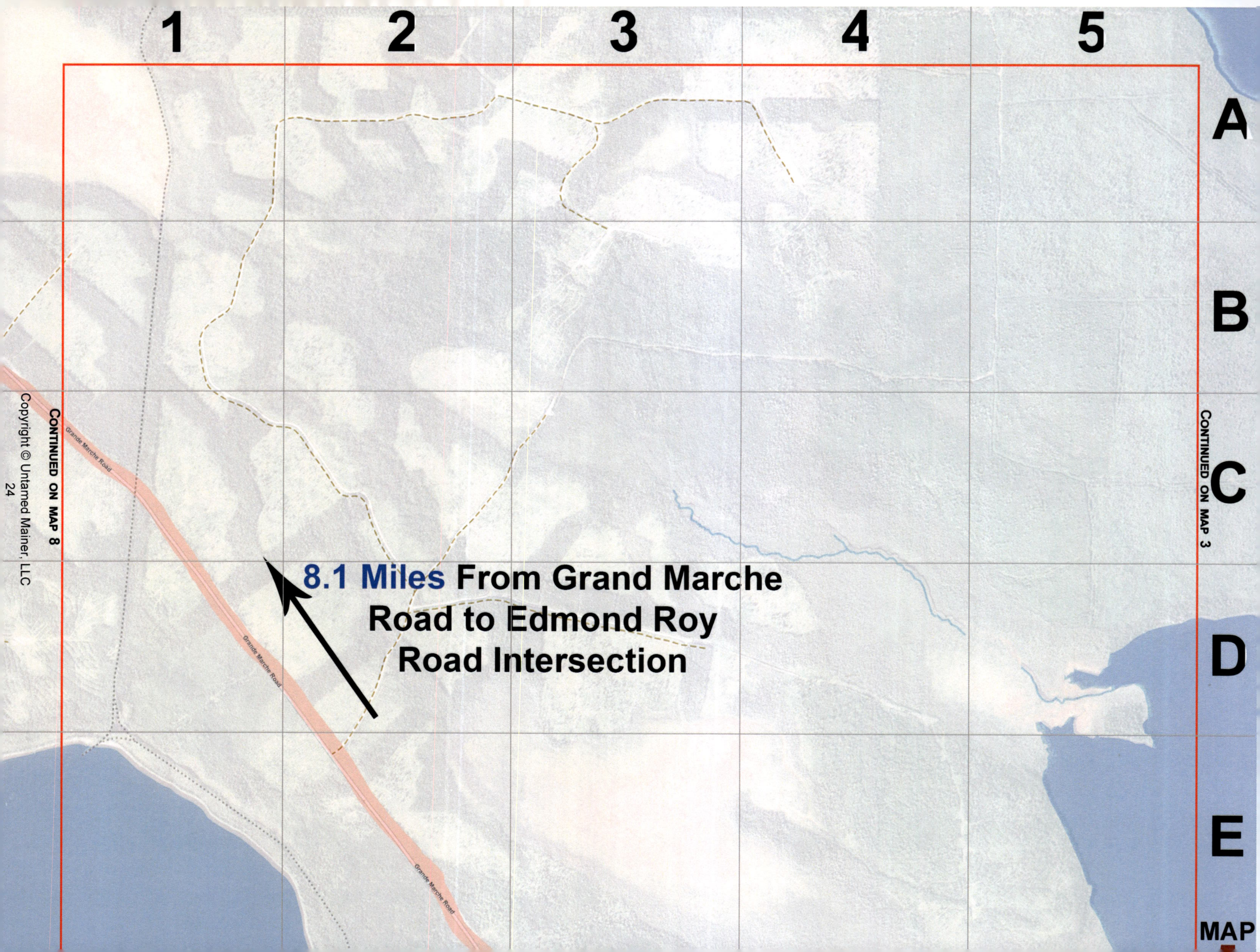

1
2
3
4
5
A
B
C
D
E
MAP
CONTINUED ON MAP 3
CONTINUED ON MAP 8
8.1 Miles From Grand Marche Road to Edmond Roy Road Intersection
Grande Marche Road
Grande Marche Road

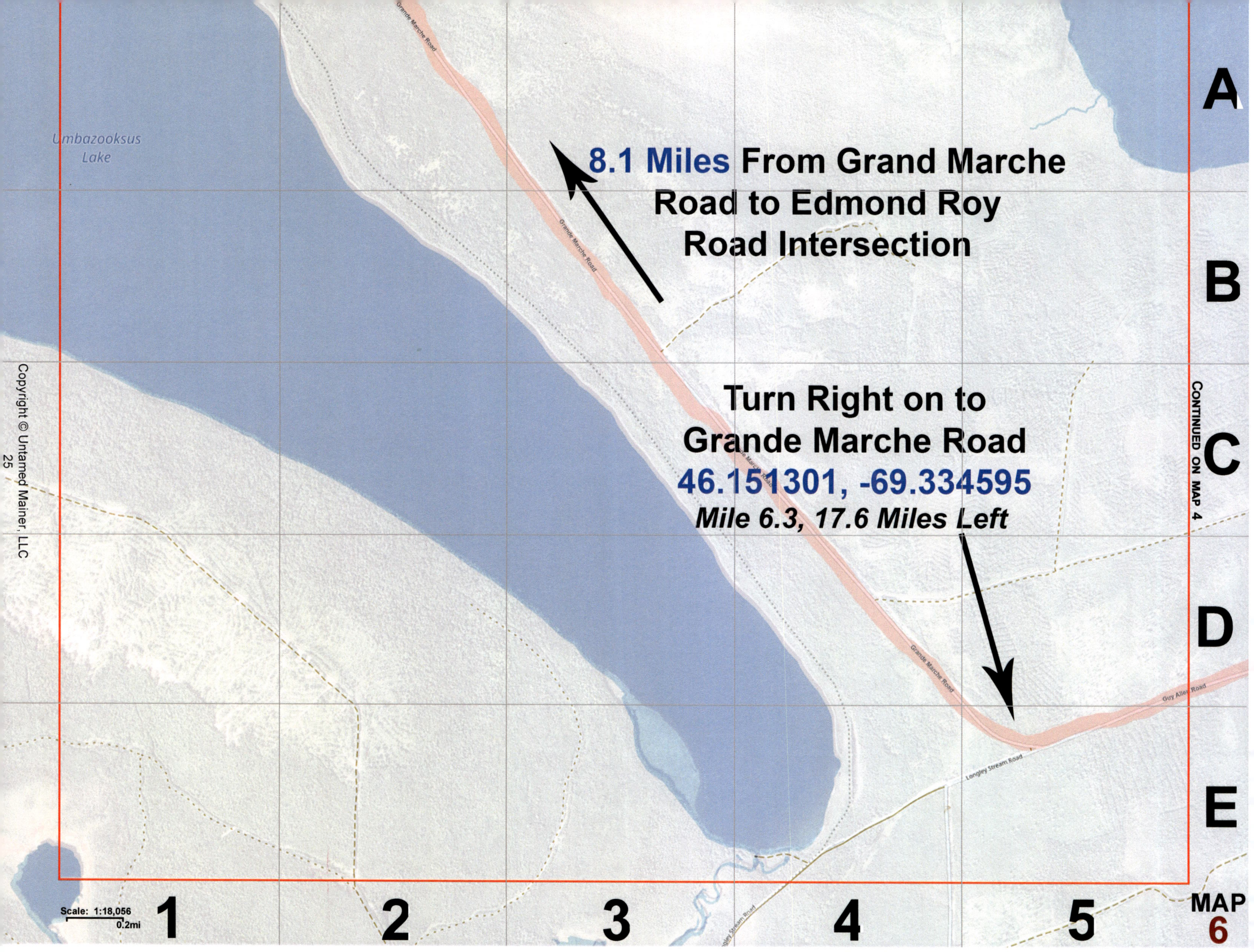

MAP 6
8.1 Miles From Grand Marche
Road to Edmond Roy
Road Intersection
Turn Right on to
Grande Marche Road
46.151301, -69.334595
Mile 6.3, 17.6 Miles Left
CONTINUED ON MAP 4
Grande Marche Road
Guy Allie Road
Longley Stream Road
Umbazooksus Lake
Scale: 1:18,056
0.2mi

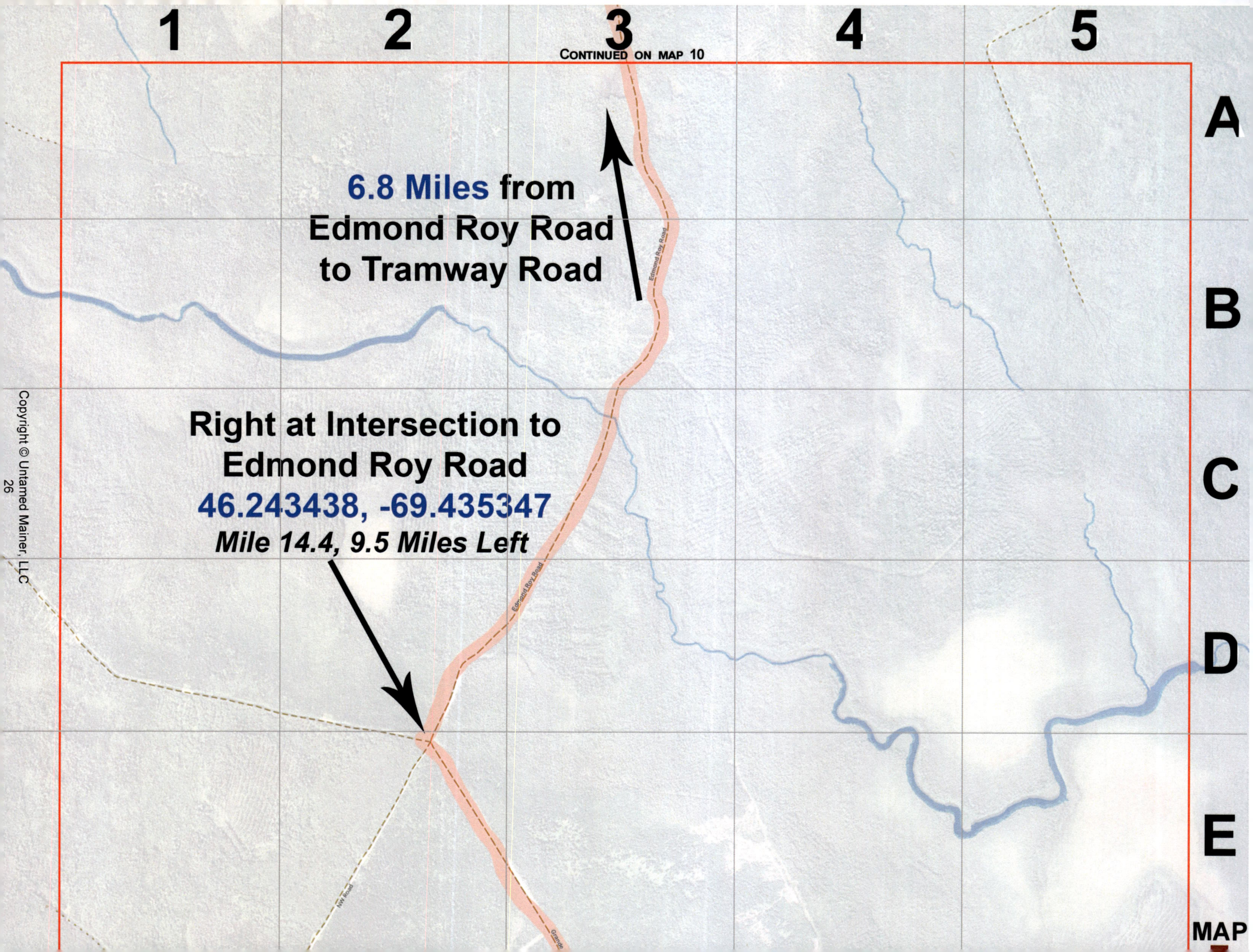
1   2   3   4   5
CONTINUED ON MAP 10
A
B
C
D
E
MAP
6.8 Miles from
Edmond Roy Road
to Tramway Road
Right at Intersection to
Edmond Roy Road
46.243438, -69.435347
Mile 14.4, 9.5 Miles Left
Edmond Roy Road
HW Road
Grande

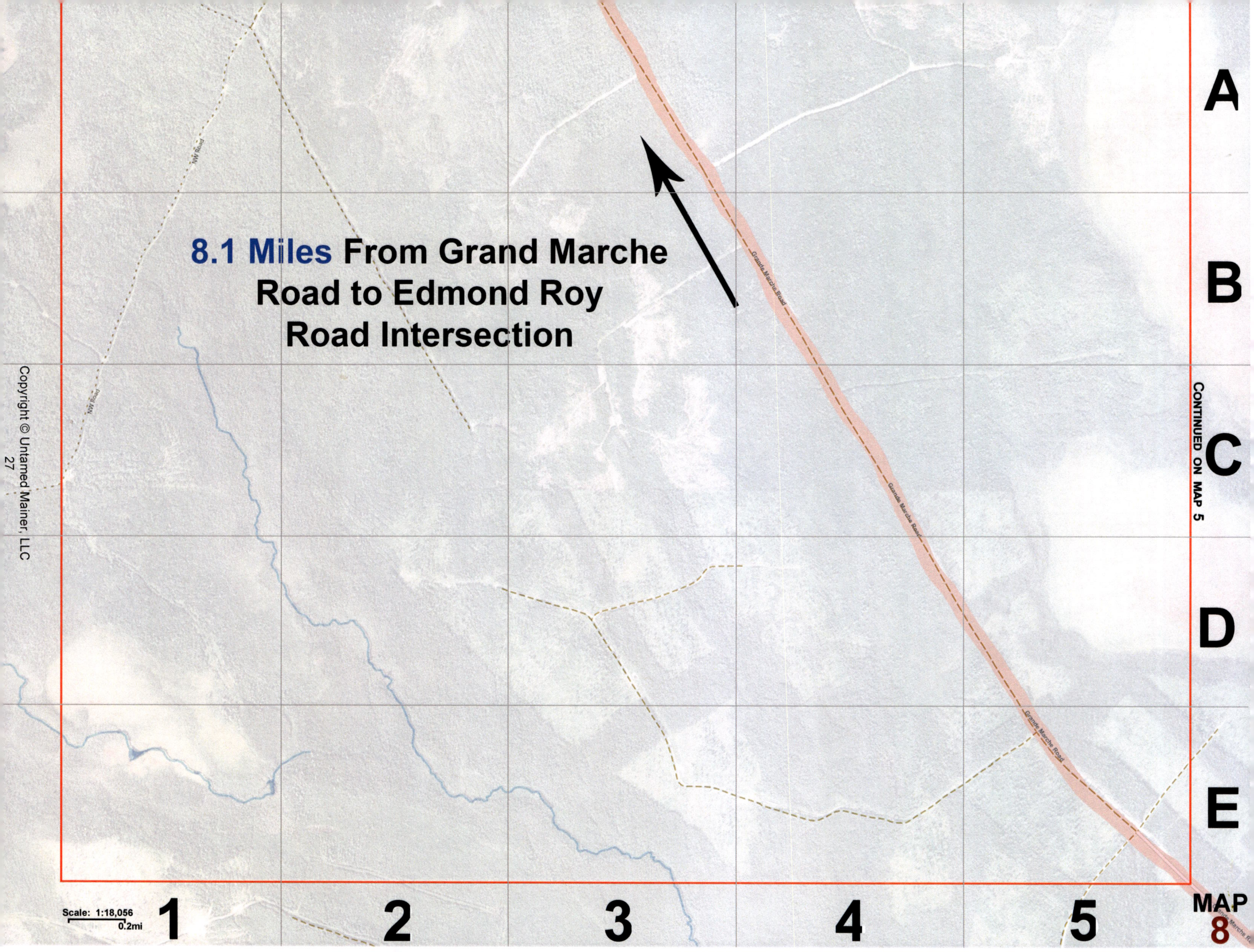

8.1 Miles From Grand Marche Road to Edmond Roy Road Intersection
Grande Marche Road
CONTINUED ON MAP 5
MAP 8
A
B
C
D
E
1
2
3
4
5
Scale: 1:18,056
0.2mi

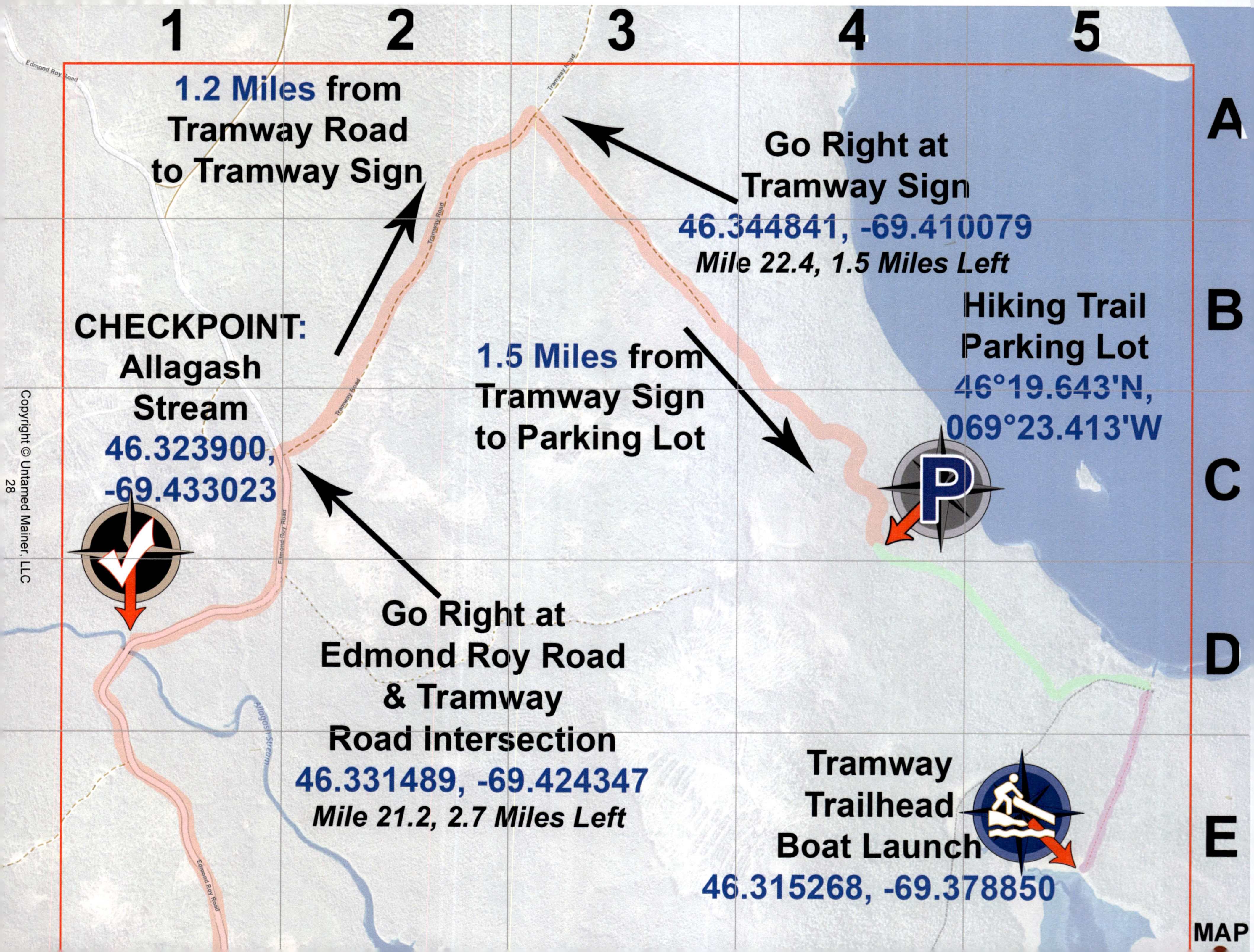

1   2   3   4   5
A   B   C   D   E
MAP
1.2 Miles from Tramway Road to Tramway Sign
Go Right at Tramway Sign
46.344841, -69.410079
Mile 22.4, 1.5 Miles Left
Hiking Trail Parking Lot
46°19.643'N, 069°23.413'W
CHECKPOINT: Allagash Stream
46.323900, -69.433023
1.5 Miles from Tramway Sign to Parking Lot
Go Right at Edmond Roy Road & Tramway Road Intersection
46.331489, -69.424347
Mile 21.2, 2.7 Miles Left
Tramway Trailhead Boat Launch
46.315268, -69.378850
Copyright © Untamed Mainer, LLC
28

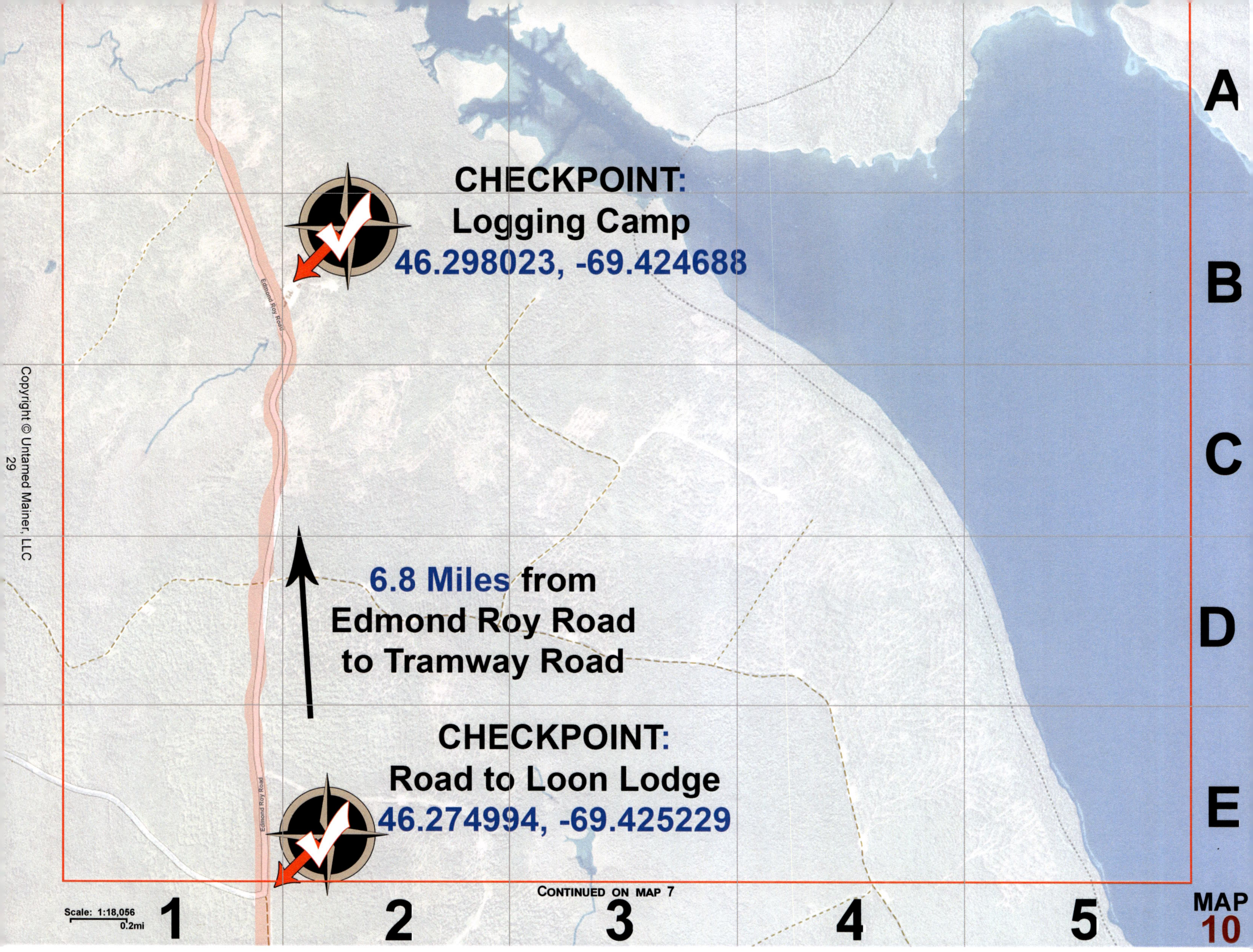
A
B
C
D
E
1
2
3
4
5
MAP
10
CHECKPOINT:
Logging Camp
46.298023, -69.424688
6.8 Miles from
Edmond Roy Road
to Tramway Road
CHECKPOINT:
Road to Loon Lodge
46.274994, -69.425229
CONTINUED ON MAP 7
Edmond Roy Road
Scale: 1:18,056
0.2mi
Copyright © Untamed Mainer, LLC
29

Hiking Trail & Conditions

This is the parking lot where you'll start hiking. There is an outhouse to the far left of the photo. Although there was toilet paper in it when I was there, you might want to bring your own just in case. The trailhead is where you see the sign next to the vehicle on the right side of the photo. The trail is clearly marked with BLUE blaze the entire way and takes about **20-25 minutes to reach the locomotives.**

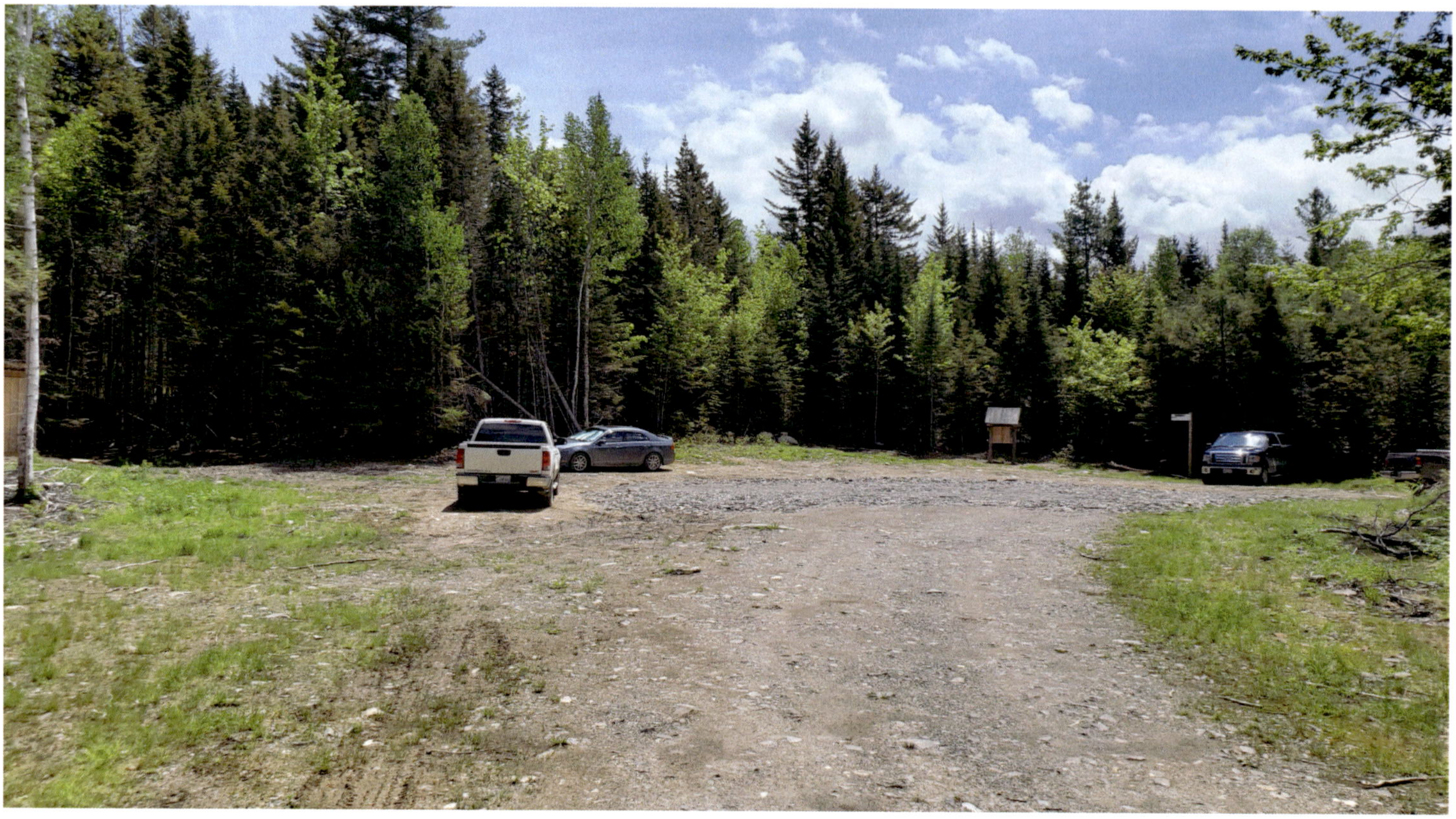

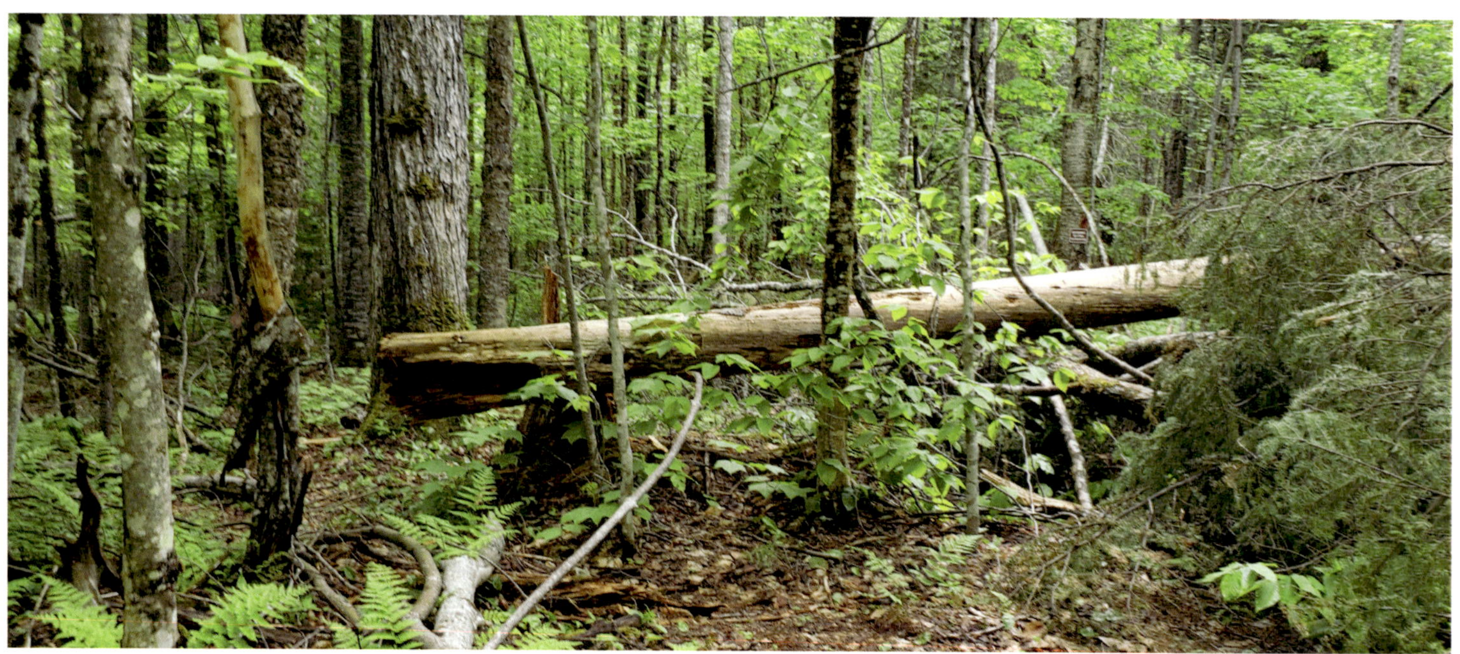

There were several trees that had fallen across the trail when we visited the locomotives like this one below. It can be a bit difficult to see where the trail goes next when going around them, but **keep looking for the blue blazes on the trees.**

There is one tricky part to the trail where you will reach another road that has orange flagging tape. This photo is looking back towards where you came from on the left side of the photo. The trail/road on the right side of the photo is NOT where you want to go. The blue blazed trail continues **across** the orange flagged road.

You'll know you're getting close when you make a sharp turn and start walking along a high banking that **follows the train tracks** to your right in the gully below.

HIKING TRAIL & CONDITIONS

Eventually you'll cross the tracks in the gully and meet up with where the **original hiking trail to the locomotives** was, shown in the picture below. The old trail came in from the left hand side of the photo.

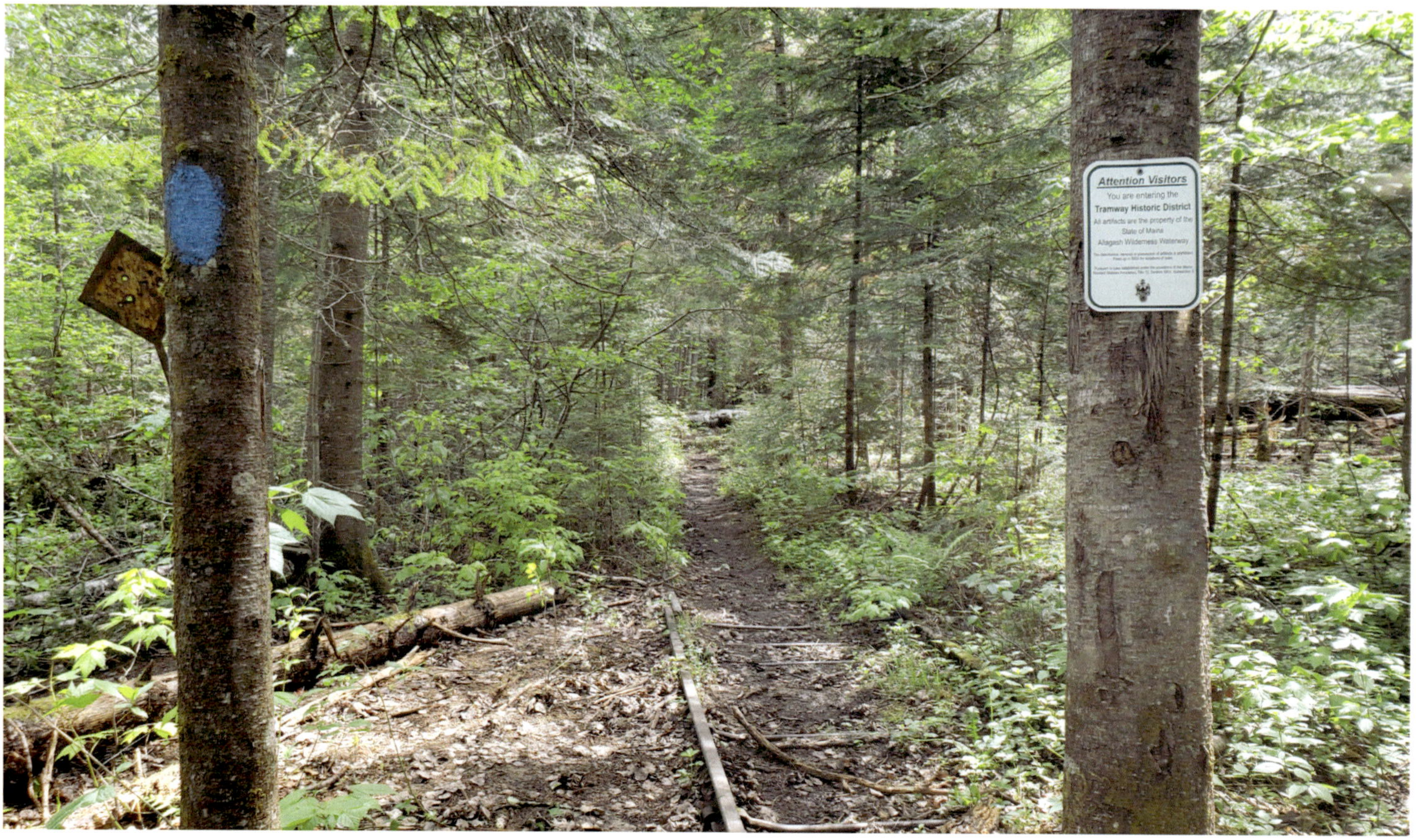

From there you'll follow the tracks all the way to the locomotives!

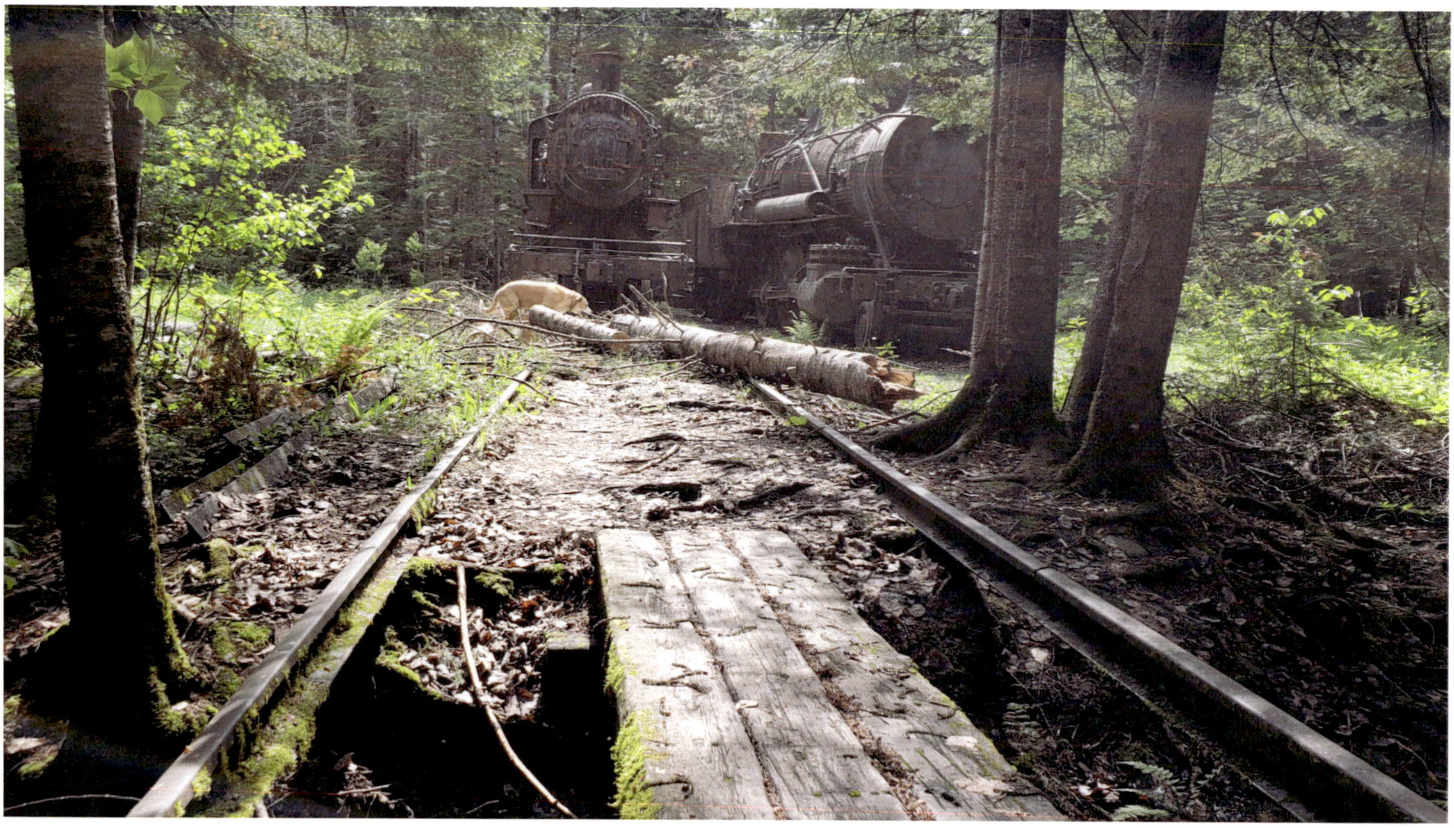

Hiking Trail and Tramway Historic District Maps

The hiking trail map to the locomotives is on the following pages. The aerial map below shows where the other map pages are located in reference to one another. The hiking trail from the parking lot to the locomotives is highlighted in **GREEN**. The red square on the map is where map page 1 and 2 overlap. The **PURPLE** highlighted trail is the portage trail for paddlers and also leads to the log conveyor and remains of the Tramway drive machinery, boilers and engine. The purple trail is approximately 0.5 miles (half-mile) long. GPS coordinates are given for important locations on the map, including historical features and artifacts. **GPS coordinates are given in a different format in the *Key Features of Tramway Historic District* section.** Photos of these locations follow the map pages.

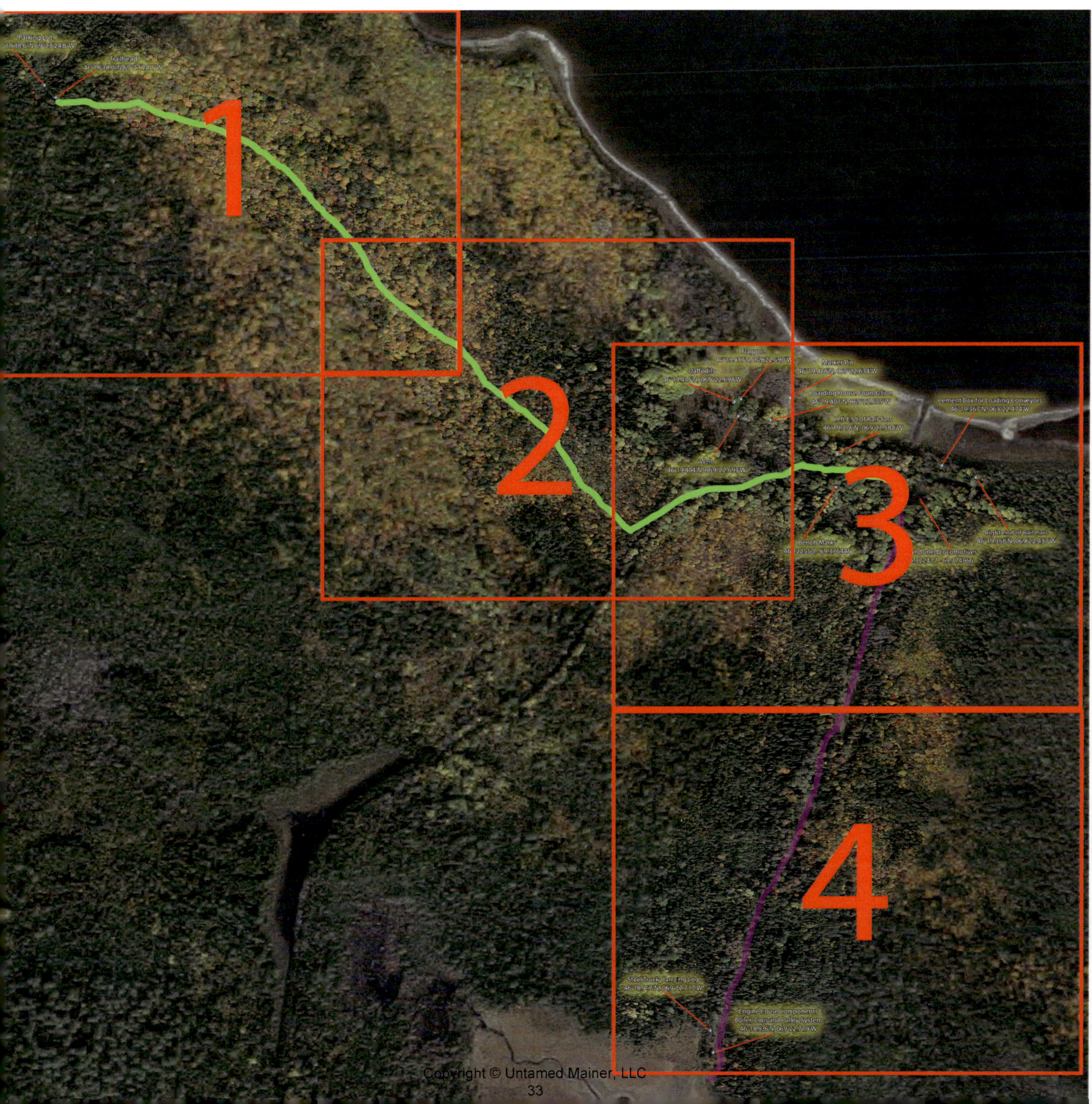

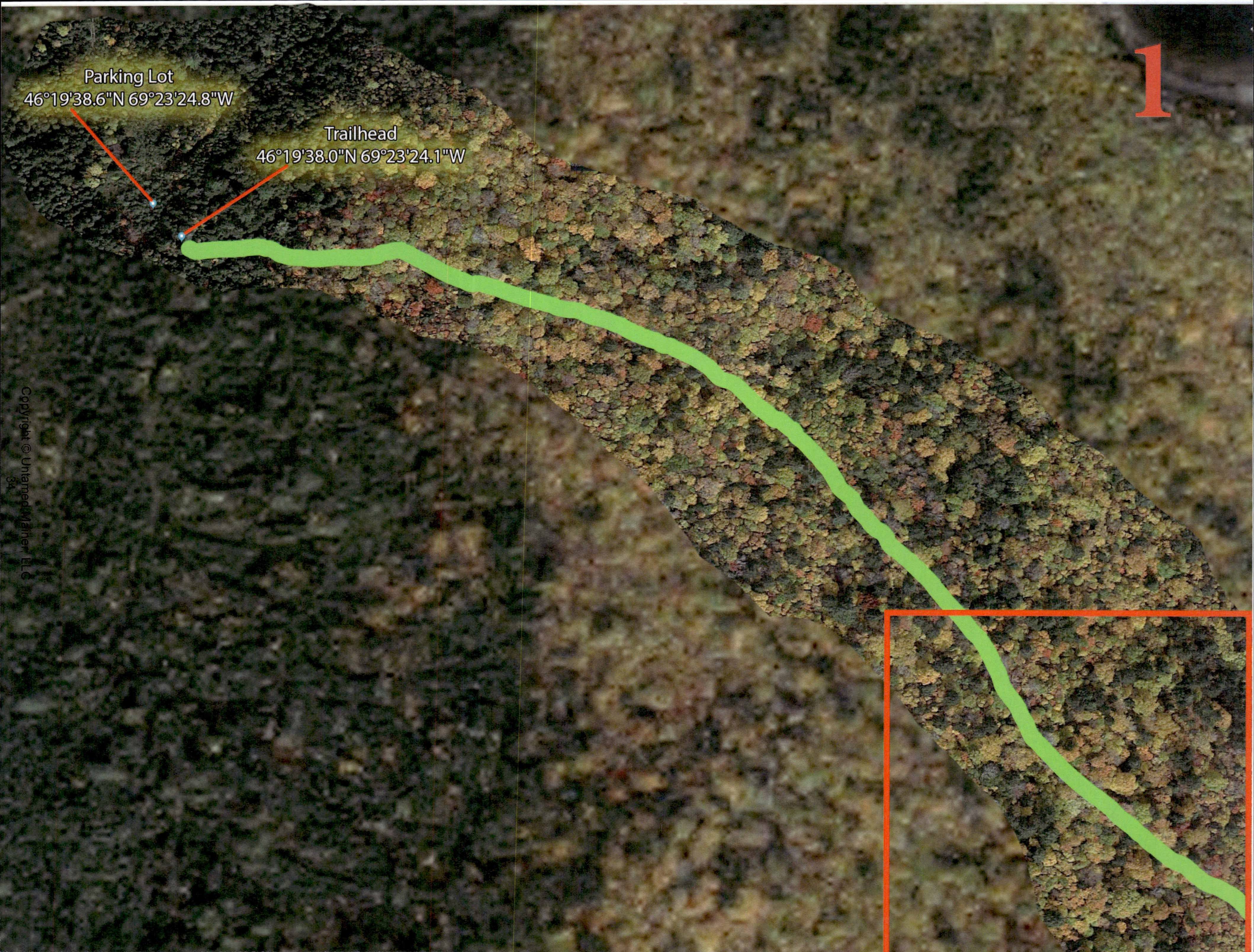

1
Parking Lot
46°19'38.6"N 69°23'24.8"W
Trailhead
46°19'38.0"N 69°23'24.1"W

Flagpole
46°19.417'N, 069°22.690'W
Daffodils
46°19.415'N, 069°22.698'W
Well
46°19.404'N, 069°22.693'W
2

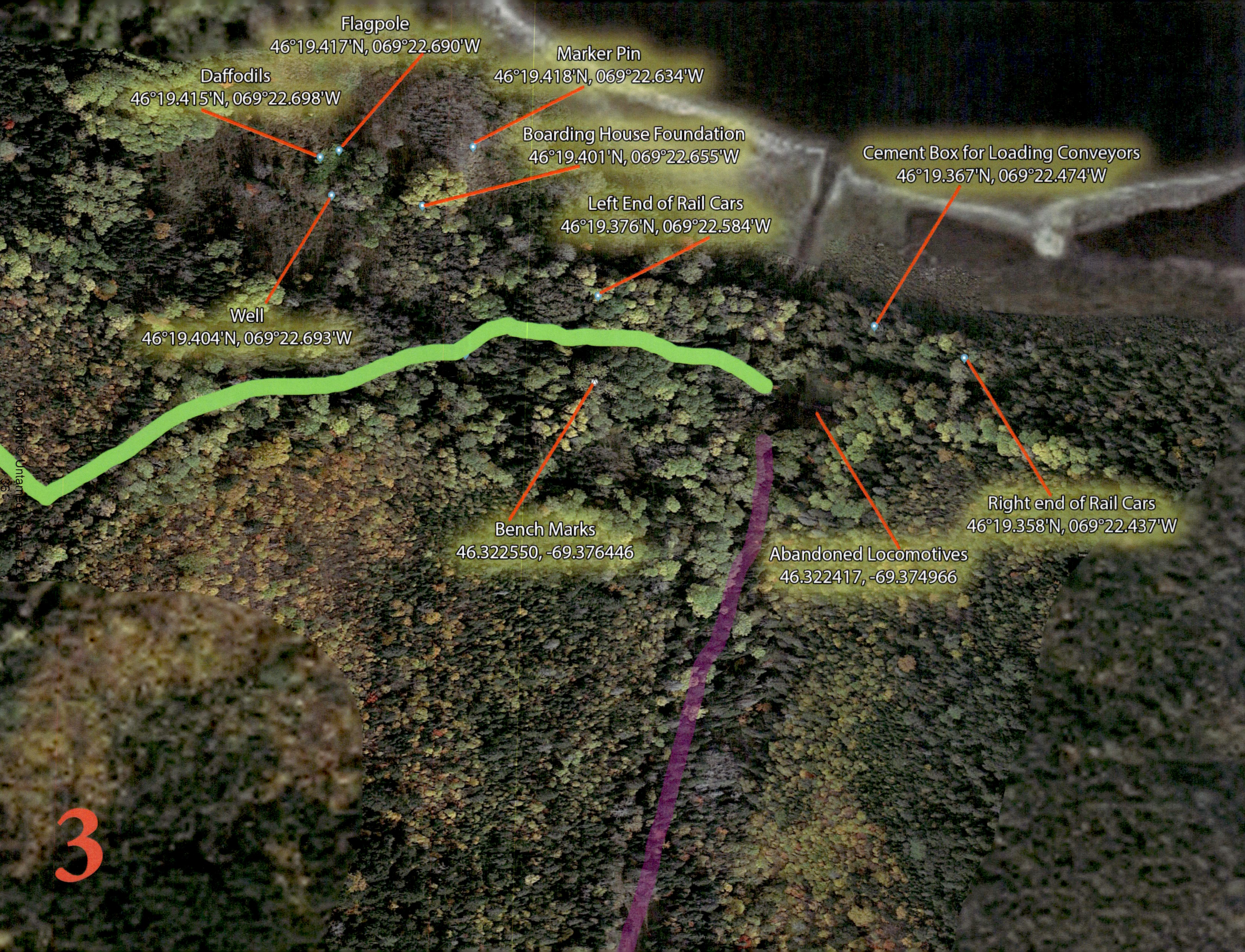

Flagpole
46°19.417'N, 069°22.690'W
Daffodils
46°19.415'N, 069°22.698'W
Marker Pin
46°19.418'N, 069°22.634'W
Boarding House Foundation
46°19.401'N, 069°22.655'W
Cement Box for Loading Conveyors
46°19.367'N, 069°22.474'W
Left End of Rail Cars
46°19.376'N, 069°22.584'W
Well
46°19.404'N, 069°22.693'W
Bench Marks
46.322550, -69.376446
Abandoned Locomotives
46.322417, -69.374966
Right end of Rail Cars
46°19.358'N, 069°22.437'W
3

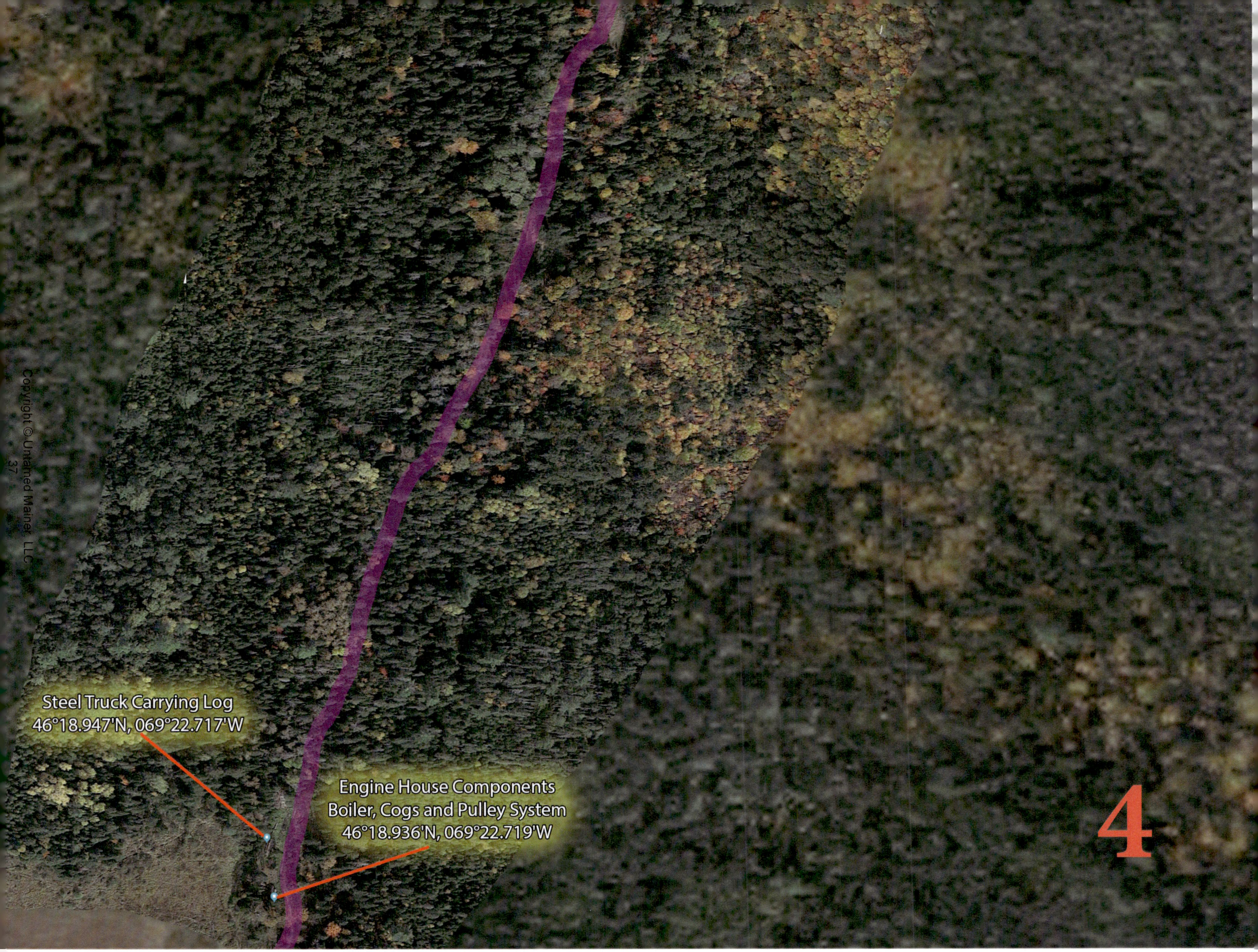

Steel Truck Carrying Log
46°18.947'N, 069°22.717'W
Engine House Components
Boiler, Cogs and Pulley System
46°18.936'N, 069°22.719'W
4

Abandoned Locomotives
GPS Coordinates: 46.322417, -69.374966

Pulp Rail Cars
GPS Coordinates: Left end 46.322941, -69.376403, Right end 46.322633, -69.373950

Cement Box/Footing for Loading Conveyors
GPS Coordinates: 46.322783, -69.374567

Boarding House Foundation
GPS Coordinates: 46.323350, -69.377583

Marker Pin, unknown purpose
GPS Coordinates: 46.323633, -69.377233

Forest Service Camp Flagpole
GPS Coordinates: 46.323617, -69.378167

Daffodils, Old Forest Service Camp Grounds
GPS Coordinates: 46.323583, -69.378300

Well (closed, don't walk on the logs, they aren't stable!)
GPS Coordinates: 46.323400, -69.378217

Well (open carefully, logs are flimsy, Please close the well back up to preserve it)

Key Features of Tramway Historical District

teel Trucks Transporting a Log

PS Coordinates: 46.315783, -69.378617

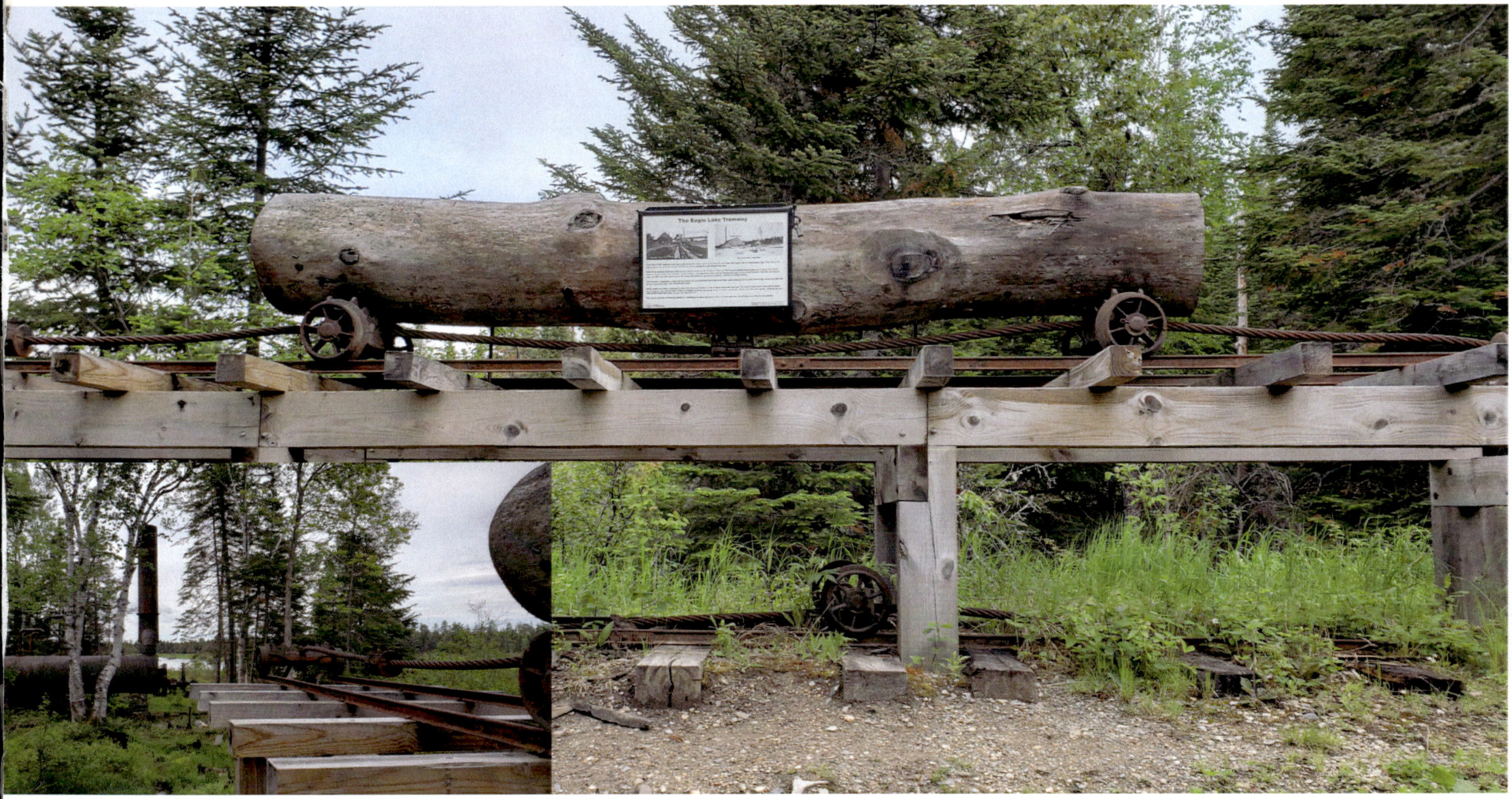

ngine House Components, Engine, Cogs, & Pulley System

PS Coordinates: 46.315600, -69.378650

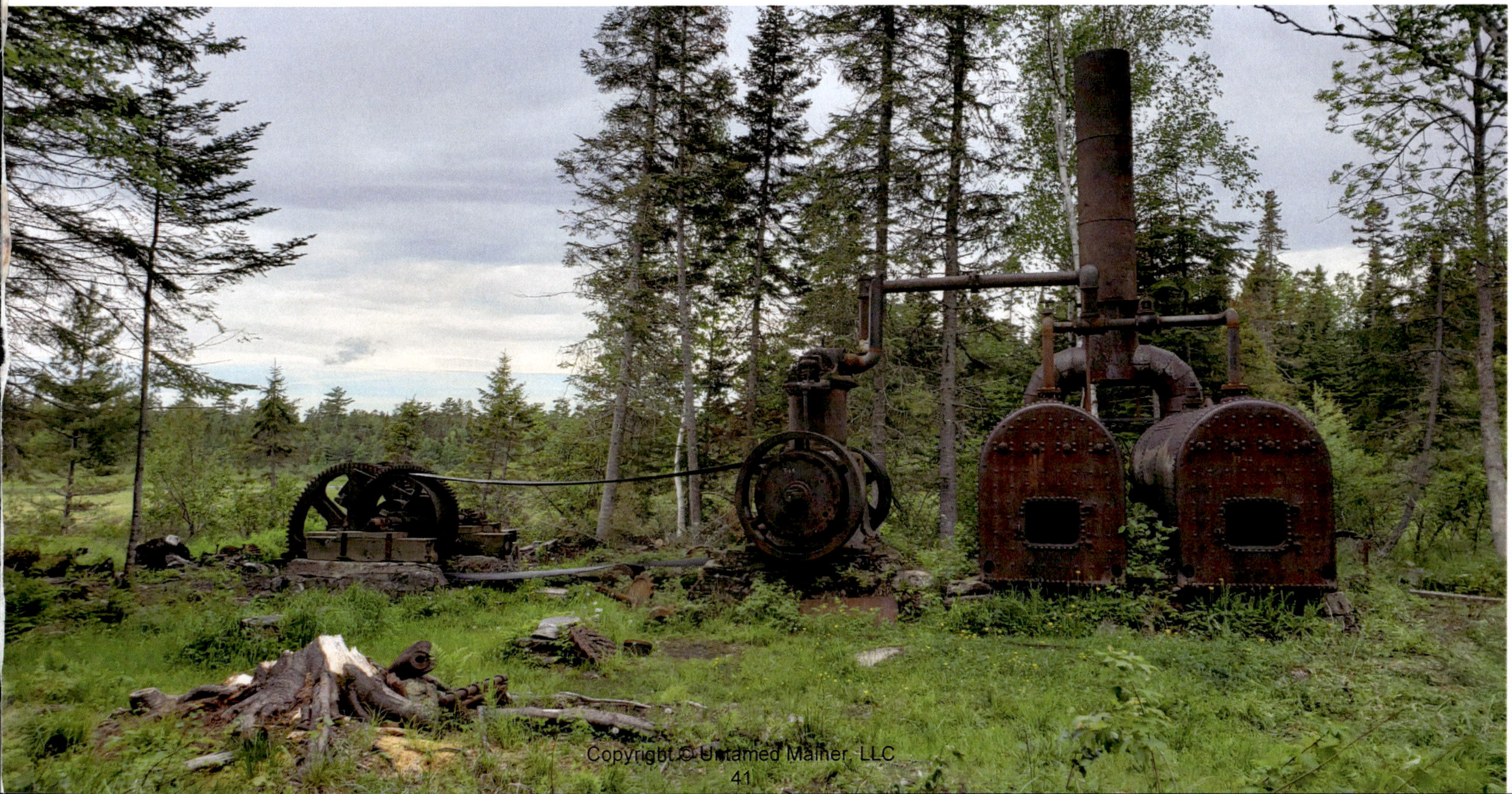

www.ingramcontent.com/pod-product-compliance
Lightning Source LLC
Chambersburg PA
CBRC090747110726
48005CB00008B/987